FISH 魚

CHINESE STYLE MADE EASY

Pescado Estilo Chino Fácil de Preparar

味全食譜
Wei-Chuan Cookbook

總編輯
黃淑惠

編輯
邱澄子

作者
李木村
陳雪霞

食譜提供
許文舜
洪柏惟
伍　明
林茂盛

文稿協助
陳素真
蔡壽蓮
陳寶妃
蔣瑞容
賴燕貞
何久恩
李愛茜

英文翻譯
蕭杏如

西文翻譯
安保羅
安西雅
馬利亞

設計編輯
張方馨
汪金光

攝影
大野現
吳華勝
章靄琳
江文榮

封面設計
王　錦

電腦排版
精美印前輸出資訊中心

分色製版
福茂彩色製版有限公司

印刷
錦龍印刷實業股份有限公司

味全出版社有限公司
台北市仁愛路四段28號2樓
電話：2702-1148．2702-1149
傳真：2704-2729
郵政劃撥00182038號
味全出版社帳戶

版權所有：
局版台業字第0179號
中華民國87年2月初版
定價：新台幣參佰元整

EDITOR
Su-Huei Huang

ASSOCIATE EDITOR
Cheng-Tzu Chiu

AUTHORS
Mu-Tsun Lee
Hsueh-Hsia Chen

RECIPES
Wen-Shun Hsu
Po-Wei Hung
Ming Wu
Mao-Sheng Lin

EDITORIAL STAFF
Su-Jen Chen
Shou-Lien Tsai
Pao-Fei Chen
Ruth Chiang
Yen-Jen Lai
John Holt
Elsa Lee

ENGLISH TRANSLATION
Bernadette Hsin Burkhead

SPANISH TRANSLATION
Paul Andersen
Sylvia Jimenez-Andersen
Maria Teresa Aguirre

ART DIRECTION
F. S. Chang
Chin-Kuang Wang

PHOTOGRAPHY
Aki Ohno
Hua-Sheng Wu
Irene Chang
William Chiang

COVER DESIGN
Chin Ong

PRINTED IN TAIWAN, R.O.C.
JIN LONG PRINTING &
STATIONERY CO., LTD.

WEI-CHUAN PUBLISHING
1455 Monterey Pass Road, #110
Monterey Park, CA 91754, U.S.A.
Tel: 213-261-3880
Fax: 213-261-3299

FIRST PRINTING, FEBRUARY 1998
ISBN 0-941676-72-2
(English/Chinese/Spanish)

EDITOR
Su-Huei Huang

EDITORA ADJUNTA
Cheng-Tzu Chiu

AUTORES
Mu-Tsun Lee
Hsueh-Hsia Chen

RECETAS
Wen-Shun Hsu
Po-Wei Huang
Ming Wu
Mao-Sheng Lin

ASISTENTES DEL EDITOR
Su-Jen Chen
Shou-Lien Tsai
Pao-Fei Chen
Ruth Chiang
Yen-Jen Lai
John Holt
Elsa Lee

TRADUCCIÓN AL INGLÉS
Bernadette Hsin Burkhead

TRADUCCIÓN AL ESPAÑOL
Paul Andersen
Sylvia Jiménez Andersen
Maria Teresa Aguirre

DIRECCIÓN ARTÍSTICA
F. S. Chang
Chin-Kuang Wang

FOTOGRAFIA
Aki Ohno
Hua-Sheng Wu
Irene Chang
William Chiang

DISEÑO DE LA PORTADA
Ching Ong

IMPRESO EN TAIWAN, R.O.C.
JIN LONG PRINTING &
STATIONERY CO., LTD.

WEI-CHUAN PUBLISHING
1455 Monterey Pass Road, #110
Monterey Park, CA 91754, U.S.A.
Tel: 213-261-3880
Fax: 213-261-3299

DERECHOS © 1998
Por Wei-Chuan Publishing
Todos los derechos están reservados. No se puede reproducir parte alguna de este libro por ningún motivo sin autorización del editor.

Aviso: De acuerdo a lo mejor de nuestro conocimiento la información contenida en este libro es completa y correcta. Todas las recomendaciones están hechas sin garantías por parte del autor de la compañía Wei-Chuan. El autor y editor rechazan toda la responsabilidad en conección con el uso y uso indebido de esta información.

Wei-Chuan Cooking School was founded in 1961 as a subsidiary of Wei-Chuan Food Corporation, the largest food manufacturer in Taiwan. The school soon became the largest and most respected institution of its kind along the Asia-Pacific rim. Graduates include world-class chefs, institutional teachers, professional caterers, connoisseurs of Chinese and international cuisines as well as many homemakers.

As Wei-Chuan's reputation grew, requests came from all over the world for guidance and information relative to the recipes used in the cooking classes. In an effort to meet this demand, **Chinese Cuisine** was written and published in 1972. The book was very successful and became the first in a series of Wei-Chuan Cookbooks. Wei-Chuan Publishing was founded later that same year in Taipei with a branch subsequently established in the U.S.A. in 1978.

Wei-Chuan, long recognized as publishing the most comprehensive Chinese cuisine cookbooks, has now expanded its recipes to include other cuisines from around the world.

Wei-Chuan's success can be attributed to its commitment to provide the best quality product possible. All recipes are complemented by full color photographs. Each recipe is written simply with easy-to-follow instructions and precisely measured ingredients. Wei-Chuan stands behind its name, reputation, and commitment to remain true to the authenticity of its recipes.

La Escuela de Cocina Wei-Chuan fue fundada en 1961 como subsidiaria de Wei-Chuan Food Corporation, fabricante de comida más grande en Taiwán. La escuela pronto se convirtió en la institución más grande y respetada de su clase en el aro del Pacífico-Asiático. Nuestros graduados incluyen chefs reconocidos mundialmente, profesores institucionales, abastecedores profesionales y conocedores de cocina china como también amas de casa.

Mientras la reputación de Wei-Chuan creció, se recibían solicitudes de todas partes del mundo pidiendo consejos e información pertinentes a las recetas usadas en las clases de cocina. En un esfuerzo para satisfacer este requerimiento, **Chinese Cuisine** *fue escrito y publicado en 1972. El libro fue un gran éxito y el primero en una serie de Libros de Cocina de Wei-Chuan. La casa editorial Wei-Chuan fue fundada, luego ese mismo año en Taipeh, seguida por una sucursal establecida en E.U. en 1978.*

Los libros de cocina Wei-Chuan ahora se reconocen como los libros más completos en el campo de la cocina china. Los proyectos presentes de Wei-Chuan incluyen nuevos libros que cubren la cocina de todo el mundo.

El éxito de Wei-Chuan se debe a su compromiso en proveer el producto de más alta calidad posible. Casi todas las recetas se complementan con fotografías a todo color. Cada receta está escrita con instrucciones fáciles de seguir y con ingredientes meticulosamente medidos. Wei-Chuan respalda su nombre, su reputación y su compromiso en mantenerse fiel a la autenticidad de sus recetas.

Table of Contents 目　錄 *Contenido*

Conversion Table · 量器介紹 · *Tabla de Conversión*

1 cup (1 c.) = 236 c.c
1杯(1飯碗)=16大匙   *taza (tz.)*

1 tablespoon (1 T.) = 15 c.c.
1大匙(1湯匙)   *cucharada (C.)*

1 teaspoon (1 t.) = 5 c.c.
1小匙(1茶匙)   *cucharadita (c.)*

序 本公司於民國73年推出「海鮮專輯」，內容包含李木村先生平日所蒐集的各式海鮮及海霸王、海村、珍寶等三家台灣著名的海鮮餐廳名廚——許文舜、洪柏惟、伍明、林茂盛先生所提供的拿手絕活，由於內容廣泛，技巧精湛，出書以來廣受海內外讀者的喜愛，也因而促使我們更積極地投入與鑽研，期望能提供海鮮愛好者更多更簡便的海鮮新口味。

本書取材自原「海鮮專輯」中的魚類部份，再加入陳雪霞老師於其20餘年的烹飪教學中精選易做而又適合現代人的魚類烹調精華彙編而成，無論在選材或製作上都極富變化，使讀者能充份掌握魚類清鮮甘美的特性，烹調時更得心應手，讓家人品嚐您點點滴滴的愛意，增添生活無盡的樂趣。

李木村先生現任日本神戶「李魚翅海鮮中國菜館」主理，著有「速簡中國菜」。
陳雪霞老師現任中國文化大學生活應用科學系講師，著有「均衡飲食」及「實用家庭菜」。

本公司與「魚」專輯同時推出姊妹作——「蝦貝蟹」專輯，以饗讀者。

Introduction

In 1984, we published "Chinese Seafood" co-authored by the famous teacher and chef Mr. Mu-Tsun Lee and by Mr. Wen-Shun Hsu, Po-Wei Hung, Ming Wu, and Mao-Sheng Lin, the chefs of Taiwan's most famous seafood restaurants: "Hai Pa Wang", "Hai Tsun", and "Jumbo". Since "Chinese Seafood" became such a hit, it prompted us to research seafood in depth to offer seafood lovers more and simple-to-make seafood dishes.

The Fish Section of "Chinese Seafood" has been incorporated into this book. In addition, the elite among Ms. Hsueh-Hsia Chen's 20-year fish cooking collection from her teaching profession have been added into this book. The ingredients and procedures are so versatile and easy-to-follow that they readily suit the life style of contemporary people. Seafood lovers can savor the fresh and delicious tastes of homemade fish dishes. Mr. Mu-Tsun Lee is currently the master chef of "Lee's Garden Seafood Chinese Restaurant" in Japan and the author of "Chinese Cooking Made Easy". Ms. Hsueh-Hsia Chen is currently a veteran teacher in the Applied Life Science Department of the Chinese Cultural University in Taiwan. "Shellfish" is another seafood book we offer as a companion to this text which meets the highest expectations of the most discriminating seafood lover.

Introducción

En 1984, publicamos "Chinese Seafood" escrito por el famoso maestro y chef Sr. Mu-Tsun Lee y por Sr. Wen-Shun Hsu, Po-Wei Hung, Ming Wu, y Mao-Sheng Lin, los chefs del los restaurantes más famosos de Taiwán: "Hai Pa Wang", "Hai Tsun" y "Jumbo". Desde que "Chinese Seafood" se convirtió en un gran éxito nos motivamos a investigar la comida del mar más detalladamente para ofrecer a los aficionados al marisco más platillos de mariscos y pescado fáciles de preparar.

La sección de pescado de "Chinese Seafood" ha sido incorporada en este libro. Además, se ha agregado la mejor colección de cocina de pescado de la carrera educativa de 20 años de la Sra. Hsueh-Hsia Chen. Los ingredientes y procedimientos son tan versátiles y fáciles de preparar que pueden ajustarse a la vida diaria de personas contemporáneas. Los aficionados al marisco pueden gozar de los sabores frescos y deliciosos de platillos de pescado caseros. Hoy en día el Sr. Mu-Tsun Lee es el chef maestro de "Lee's Garden Seafood Chinese Restaurant" en el Japón y es el autor de "Comida China Fácil de Preparar" y la Sra. Hsueh-Hsia Chen es una profesora veterana en el departamento de Ciencias Naturales Aplicadas en la Universidad Cultural China en Taiwán. "Mariscos", otro libro de cocina del mar que ofrecemos, acompaña muy bien este texto puesto que también satisface los gustos finos del aficionado al marisco más exigente.

Preparación de Pescado

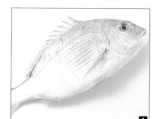

1. 新鮮魚類的選擇要領　新鮮的魚肉堅實而富彈性，選擇時宜注意
   1. 眼睛明亮，魚鱗緊貼，魚肚無破損（圖1）。
   2. 鰓鮮紅，肉質有彈性且沒有異味。
   3. 切片的魚肉需紋路清晰而有光澤。

2. 魚的處理法
   1. 魚鱗刮除乾淨，由腹部剖開。
   2. 將鰓與魚頭下巴連接處切開，取出鰓及內臟。
   3. 魚洗淨瀝乾，調醃料，如採煎、炸法，烹調前應再拭乾水份，以防油爆。
   4. 魚身較厚的魚可在兩面各劃刀再烹煮，較易熟而入味。

3. 魚肉的切割法
   1. 魚取肉時先切下頭部（圖2），再由背部下刀（圖3），順大骨切開（圖4）。
   2. 取肉，將腹部的肉切除（圖5），因魚腹肉薄多刺且有腥味。
   3. 去皮（圖6），同法取下另一邊的肉。
   4. 切魚片、魚條時均應順著紋路切，才不易散開。

1. **Tips for Buying Whole Fresh Fish**　Fresh fish are firm to the touch. Look for :
   1. bright eyes, tightly attached scales, and an intact belly (Fig. 1).
   2. bright red gills, meat texture is firm, and no fetid odor.
   3. clear grain on shiny flesh.

2. **Techniques for Preparing Fish**
   1. Scale fish thoroughly and cut along the belly.
   2. Make a cut between the head and gills. Remove and discard gills and entrails.
   3. Rinse the fish, pat dry, then marinate with sauces. Pat dry again before pan-frying to prevent oil from spattering while frying.
   4. Score the flesh in the thick areas on both sides so it will absorb the sauces more easily and cook through quickly.

3. **Techniques for Filleting**
   1. Cut off the head before filleting (Fig. 2); slice from the tail toward the head (Fig. 3) by sliding the blade along the backbone (Fig. 4).
   2. Remove the fillets from both sides (Fig. 5); cut off and discard the flesh around the belly for it not only contains bones, but has a fetid odor.
   3. Remove skin (Fig. 6). Repeat on the other side to remove the fillet.
   4. When cutting fillets into slices or strips, cut with the grain of the fish to prevent the meat from breaking up.

1. ***SUGERENCIAS PARA COMPRAR PESCADO FRESCO ENTERO***　*El pescado fresco es sólido al tocarse. Busque pescado que tenga:*
   1. *ojos claros y escamas y estómago intactos (Fig. 1).*
   2. *branquias rojas brillantes, textura de carne firme, y no olor fétido,*
   3. *la superficie granulosa clara sobre la piel brillante.*

2. ***MÉTODOS PARA PREPARAR EL PESCADO***
   1. *Descame el pescado completamente y haga un corte por el estómago.*
   2. *Haga un corte entre la cabeza y branquias. Saque y tire las branquias y entrañas.*
   3. *Enjuague el pescado, seque, y marine con salsas. Seque otra vez antes de freír en la sartén para prevenir que el aceite salpique mientras se fríe.*
   4. *Haga cortes en las áreas gruesas de la piel por ambos lados para que absorba las salsas fácilmente y se cocine total y rápidamente.*

3. ***MÉTODOS PARA CORTAR EN FILETES***
   1. *Corte la cabeza antes de filetear (Fig. 2); corte desde la cola hacia la cabeza (Fig. 3) deslizando el cuchillo por la espina dorsal (Fig. 4).*
   2. *Quite los filetes de ambos lados (Fig. 5); corte y tire la carne alrededor del estómago ya que no sólo tiene espinas, sino también un olor fétido.*
   3. *Quite la piel (Fig. 6). Repita por el otro lado para quitar el filete.*
   4. *Cuando corte los filetes en tiras o rebanadas, córtelos siguiendo la fibra del pescado para prevenir que la carne se desbarate.*

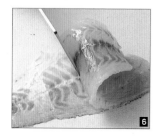

Diversos Métodos para Cocinar

烤

1 宜選油質較多或肉質較嫩者為佳,如香魚、秋刀魚、鰻魚、鮭魚、鱒魚、赤鯮、鱈魚⋯等鯮。

2 烤箱要先燒熱再烤魚以防出水,並可保持肉質的嫩度。

3 為求色澤更佳,亦可先以平底鍋煎至表面微黃,再烤至肉熟即可。

煎

1 許多魚類皆適合煎熟食用,如鮭魚、肉魚、虱目魚、帶魚、黃魚、鱈魚、鯧魚、鯕魚、鯊魚⋯等。

2 煎魚時先熱鍋再加油,油熱後倒出,另再加油燒熱後再煎,較不易沾鍋。

3 全魚或連皮魚片,可先撒些乾粉再煎較酥脆。

蒸

1 蒸魚尤要選購非常新鮮且肉嫩者為佳,如石斑魚、鱸魚、白鯧、黃魚、紅馬頭魚、鱈魚⋯等。

2 蒸魚時需用大火,待水開了魚才下鍋,至魚剛熟即可。

3 魚脂肪含量較少者,可加油或加些許肥肉來增加香味及口感。

紅燒

1 選擇肉質鮮美者即可,如赤鯮、黃魚、虱目魚、吳郭魚⋯等。

2 魚在燒煮前先煎或炸再加高湯或水及調味汁等燒煮,味道較香。

3 魚的肉質較嫩,不需燒煮太久,只要肉熟入味即可起鍋,以保持肉質鮮美。

炒

1 一般炒魚肉均切片或切條(不宜切太薄,以免破裂),故宜選肉質較不易散開者為佳,如鱸魚、鯊魚、土扥魚、鯧魚、鯕魚、石斑魚肉⋯等。

2 魚肉除以鹽、酒調味外,並應拌入太白粉,以保持滑嫩及定型。

炸

1 幾乎所有魚類皆可炸熟食用。炸魚若要酥脆些,可撒上薄薄的乾粉。

2 炸油的溫度應保持在八分熱左右效果較好,材料剛入鍋時油溫會下降,可使用大火,等溫度回升再改用中火炸(見29頁)。

煮湯

1 肉質鮮美或韌性較大的魚,如石斑魚、嘉納魚、紅目鰱、鮭魚頭、鱸魚頭或黃魚⋯等均適合煮湯。

BAKING Fatty, tender fish such as ayu or river trout, eel, salmon, trout, snapper, cod, etc are ideal for baking. Preheat oven before baking to retain fish juice and tenderness. For nice color, lightly brown fish on both sides before baking.

PAN-FRYING Salmon, Japanese butterfish, milkfish, ribbonfish, yellow croaker, cod, pomfret, sword fish, and shark are good pan-fried. To prevent fish from sticking to wok, heat wok then add oil. When oil is hot, remove oil and add new oil. Reheat oil then pan-fry. Before pan-frying flesh with skin attached or whole fish, lightly dredge fish with flour to make crispier.

STEAMING Use fresh and tender fish such as grouper, sea bass, white pomfret, yellow croaker, red horsehead, cod, etc. Steaming requires high heat. Boil water then steam fish over high heat. Remove fish immediately once done. Add a little oil or fat to a lean fish to enhance flavor and taste.

COOKING IN SOY SAUCE Snapper, yellow croaker, milkfish, mouth breeder are good for this type of cooking. To enhance flavor, pan-fry or deep-fry fish; add either stock or water then sauces; continue cooking. Since meat texture of fish is tender, do not overcook; remove fish from heat immediately once done to retain flavor and tenderness.

STIR-FRYING Fish slices or strips (do not slice too thin to prevent coming apart during cooking) are best for stir-frying. Fish, firm in texture such as sea bass, shark, barred Spanish mackerel, pomfret, sword fish, grouper, etc. are great for stir-frying. Besides salt and wine, cornstarch is also needed for marinating to firm up fish and add tenderness.

DEEP-FRYING Most fish are good for deep-frying. To make fish crispier, lightly dredge with flour before deep-frying. Maintain deep-frying oil at medium-high. When the fish first contacts oil, oil temperature drops; increase heat to high. Reduce heat to medium and continue frying process (see p. 29).

MAKING SOUP Fish, such as grouper, ghana, red bullseye, salmon head, silver carp head, or yellow croaker, etc. are ideal for making soup.

HORNEAR Pescado gordo, tierno como ayu o trucha de río, saurel, anguila, salmón, trucha, huachinango, bacalao, etc. son ideales para hornear. Precaliente el horno antes de hornear para mantener el jugo del pescado y su terneza. Para mejor color, dórelo brevemente por ambos lados antes de hornear.

FREIR EN LA SARTÉN Salmón, pampanito japonés, pez comestible, anguileta de mar, roncador amarillo, bacalao, castañola, pez espada, y tiburón son buenos para freír. Para que no se pegue en la sartén, caliente la sartén y luego agregue el aceite. Cuando el aceite esté caliente, sáquelo y agregue aceite de nuevo. Recaliente el aceite y fría. Antes de freír pescado con o sin espinas, rebócelo ligeramente con harina para hacerlo crujiente.

COCER AL VAPOR Se necesita pescado fresco y tierno como mero, róbalo, castañola blanca, roncador amarillo, bacalao, etc. Cocer al vapor requiere fuego alto. Haga hervir agua luego cueza el pescado sobre fuego alto. Saque el pescado cuando se cueza. Agregue poco aceite o grasa al pescado magro para aumentar el sabor.

COCINAR EN SALSA DE SOYA Huachinango, roncador amarillo, pez comestible, etc. son buenos para este método. Para aumentar el sabor, sofría o fría en una sartén el pescado; agregue caldo o agua luego las salsas; continúe cocinando. Ya que la textura de la carne de pescado es tierna, no lo cocine de más; saque el pescado cuando esté cocido para mantener su sabor y terneza.

FREIR-REVOLVIENDO Es mejor usar rebanadas o tiras de pescado (no las corte muy delgadas para prevenir que se desbaraten). Pescado con textura sólida como róbalo, tiburón, caballa, castañola, pez espada, mero, etc. son excelentes. Además de sal y vino, se necesita maicena para marinar el pescado y hacerlo sólido y tierno.

FREIR EN BASTANTE ACEITE Casi todos los pescado son buenos para freír en mucho aceite. Para hacer el pescado más crujiente, reboce ligeramente en harina antes de freír. Mantenga el aceite a fuego moderado alto. Cuando el pescado se pone en el aceite por primera vez, la temperatura del aceite baja. Suba el fuego a alto. Baje el fuego a mediano y continúe el procedimiento (vea p. 29).

PREPARACION DE SOPA Pescado como mero, cabeza de salmón, cabeza de carpa color plata, o roncador amarillo es ideal para hacer sopa.

烤香魚　　　　　　　Baked River Trout

Trucha de Río al Horno

4人份 · serves 4
4 porciones

香魚4條 .... 450公克（12兩）
檸檬 .... ½個
胡椒鹽 .... 隨意

① 鹽 ...... 2小匙，胡椒 ..... ¼小匙

🍃　　🍃　　🍃

4 ayu or river trout, 1 lb.
**　(450g)**
½ lemon
pepper-salt as desired

① **2 t. salt, ¼ t. pepper**

🍃　　🍃　　🍃

4 ayu o trucha de río, 1 lb.
*　(450g)*
½ limón
sal de grano de pimienta al
*　gusto*

① *2 c. sal, ¼ c. pimienta*

1️⃣ 香魚拭乾，抹上 ① 料。鰭及尾鰭部多抹些鹽以增美觀並避免燒焦。

2️⃣ 烤箱預熱至500°F（260°C），將魚放入烤約15分鐘至魚肉熟。食用時依喜好撒上檸檬汁或胡椒鹽。

☐　烤魚時，烤箱先預熱再以高溫烤或以平底鍋先煎過再入烤箱烤，則色澤佳，不易出水，可保肉質鮮嫩。

🍃　　🍃　　🍃

1️⃣ Pat the fish dry. Spread with ① . Spread more salt on fins and tail fin to prevent burning and to enhance appeal.

2️⃣ Preheat oven to 500°F (260°C). Bake fish 15 minutes until done. Serve with pepper-salt or lemon juice, if desired.

☐ Pan-fry fish in a skillet before baking to add nice color. Preheat oven then bake fish over high heat to keep the fish at its tender and juicy best.

🍃　　🍃　　🍃

1️⃣ *Seque el pescado ligeramente. Unte con ① . Unte más sal sobre las aletas y la cola para que no se quemen y para mejorar la presentación.*

2️⃣ *Precaliente el horno a 500°F (260°C). Hornee el pescado por 15 minutos hasta que esté cocido. Sirva con sal pimienta o jugo de limón, si gusta.*

☐ *Fría el pescado en una sartén antes de hornear para darle un mejor color. Precaliente el horno, luego hornee el pescado a fuego alto para mantener el pescado en su punto tierno y jugoso.*

10

烤赤鯮

Baked Snapper

Huachinango al Horno

赤鯮 .... 600公克(1斤)
鐵針（或竹籤） 1支
檸檬 .... ½個

1 酒 .... 1大匙，鹽 2小匙

  🥄   🥄   🥄

**1⅓ lbs. (600g) snapper
1 steel or wooden skewer
½ lemon**

1 | **1 T. cooking wine, 2 t. salt**

  🥄   🥄   🥄

*1⅓ lbs. (600g) huachinango
1 palillo para brochetas de
   hierro o madera
½ limón*

1 | *1 C. vino para cocinar, 2 c. sal*

1 赤鯮在肉厚處劃刀，加 **1** 料醃20分鐘，烤前瀝乾，用鐵針穿過魚身使尾部翹起，並在背胸鰭及尾鰭上抹多量鹽，則烤時不易燒焦並可做裝飾。

2 烤箱預熱至500°F（260°C），將魚放入中層烤約20分鐘至魚肉熟。食時灑檸檬汁味更佳。

烤帶魚、烤水針魚 用新鮮魚如帶魚、水針魚或香魚取代赤鯮，其餘材料及做法同上。

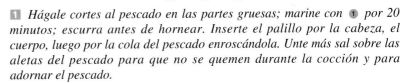

1 Score fish in thick areas; marinate in **1** for 20 minutes; drain before baking. Thread a skewer through the head, body, then tail of the fish; curl the tail. Spread more salt over the fins of the fish to prevent burning during baking and to garnish the dish.

2 Preheat oven to 500°F (260°C). Put the fish in a pan and bake it on the middle oven rack until done, about 20 minutes. For extra flavor, sprinkle lemon juice over the fish when serving.

Baked Ribbonfish, Baked Halfbeak Replace snapper with ribbonfish or halfbeak, all the other ingredients and procedures are the same as above.

  🥄   🥄   🥄

1 *Hágale cortes al pescado en las partes gruesas; marine con* **1** *por 20 minutos; escurra antes de hornear. Inserte el palillo por la cabeza, el cuerpo, luego por la cola del pescado enroscándola. Unte más sal sobre las aletas del pescado para que no se quemen durante la cocción y para adornar el pescado.*

2 *Precaliente el horno a 500°F (260°C). Coloque el pescado en un recipiente de hornear y hornéelo en la parrilla central del horno hasta que esté cocido, como 20 minutos. Para darle más sabor, rocíe jugo de limón sobre el pescado cuando lo sirva.*

Anguileta de Mar Horneada, Pescado Horneado *Substituya el huachinango con pescado fresco o anguileta de mar o el pescado horneado, los demás ingredientes y procedimientos son como lo de arriba.*

烤帶魚 · Baked Ribbonfish
Anguileta de Mar Horneada

烤水針魚 · Baked Halfback
Pescado Horneado

鋁紙烤魚　Aluminum Foil Baked Fish

Pescado Horneado en Papel de Aluminio

鮭魚或鱈魚 ..... 300公克（8兩）
鋁箔紙（30 公分×30公分）.. 1張
檸檬 2片

① 鹽 .... ½小匙
胡椒 .... ⅛小匙

② 蔥絲 2大匙
薑絲 1大匙

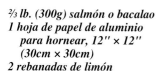

⅔ lb.(300g) salmon or codfish
1 sheet of aluminum foil for baking, 12" × 12" (30cm × 30cm)
2 lemon slices

① **½ t. salt**
⅛ t. pepper

② **2 T. shredded green onions**
1 T. shredded ginger root

⅔ lb. (300g) salmón o bacalao
1 hoja de papel de aluminio para hornear, 12" × 12" (30cm × 30cm)
2 rebanadas de limón

① *½ c. sal*
⅛ c. pimienta

② *2 C. cebollín picado*
1 C. raíz de jengibre rallada

1

2

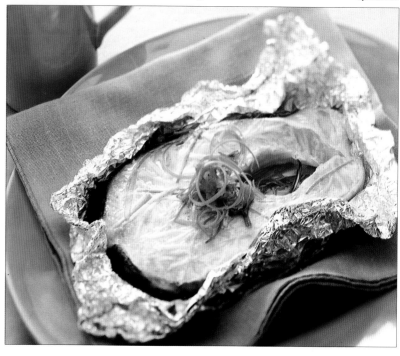

1 鮭魚切2公分厚片拭乾，抹上 **①** 料，置抹油鋁箔紙上，撒 **②** 料包妥備烤。

2 烤箱熱至450°F（230°C），放入魚烤約15分鐘至魚肉剛熟，食時依喜好撒上檸檬汁。

☐ 用鋁紙烤魚，可保留魚的鮮味與原汁。魚亦可分成四等份分別包妥（圖1、2）置冰箱中，食前15分鐘再烤即可。

1 Cut the fish into ¾" (2cm) thick slices; pat dry; spread on **①**; place on a piece of aluminum foil coated with oil; sprinkle on **②**; fold foil over fish before baking.

2 Preheat oven to 450°F (230°C). Bake fish until just done, about 15 minutes. Sprinkle on lemon juice before serving, if desired.

☐ Baking fish in aluminum foil retains its delicious flavor and juice. Also, fish can be wrapped in 4 foils (Figs. 1 & 2) and refrigerated. Bake 15 minutes before serving.

1 *Corte el pescado en rebanadas gruesas de ¾" (2cm); seque ligeramente; úntele **①**; coloque sobre la hoja de papel de aluminio untada con aceite; espolvoréele **②**; envuelva el pescado con al papel de aluminio antes de hornear.*

2 *Precaliente el horno a 450°F (230°C). Hornee el pescado hasta que esté cocido, como 15 minutos. Rocíele el jugo de limón antes de servir, si gusta.*

☐ *El hornear el pescado envuelto en aluminio hace que el pescado mantenga su delicioso sabor y su jugo. También el pescado se puede envolver en 4 pedazos de aluminio (Figs. 1 y 2) y refrigerar. Hornee por 15 minutos antes de servir.*

烤醬魚　Baked Fish with Bean Paste

Pescado Horneado con Pasta de Frijol

魚肉 .... 450公克（12兩）
檸檬 .... ½個

① 味噌或黑豆瓣醬或甜麵醬 . ½杯
糖 4大匙
酒 2大匙

❧　❧　❧

1 lb. (450g) fish fillet
½ lemon

① **½ c. miso or black bean
　paste or sweet bean
　paste**
4 T. sugar
2 T. cooking wine

❧　❧　❧

1 lb. (450g) filete de pescado
½ limón

① *½ tz. miso o pasta de frijol
　negro o pasta de frijol dulce*
4 C. azúcar
2 C. vino para cocinar

1 魚肉拭乾，切大塊，放入拌好的 ① 料內醃泡一天。

2 烤箱熱至500°F（260°C），烤盤上鋪鋁箔紙再放魚塊（先將魚塊上的醬刮除），入烤箱中層烤約12分鐘至金黃色肉熟即可，塗少許麻油，食時灑上檸檬汁味更佳。

☐ 鮭魚、鱈魚、鯧魚及黃魚等魚肉較細嫩的均可用來做烤醬魚。使用過的醬煮開待涼後可再用來泡魚。

❧　❧　❧

1 Pat fish fillets dry; cut into large pieces. Marinate the fish with mixture ① for 1 day.

2 Preheat oven to 500°F (260°C). Remove marinade from fish; place the fish on a baking pan lined with aluminum foil; bake on the middle oven rack until done and golden on both sides, about 12 minutes. Spread a little sesame oil over the fish. For extra flavor, sprinkle on lemon juice when serving.

☐ Salmon, codfish, pomfret, and yellow croaker may be used for this recipe. The leftover ingredients in ① may be saved for future use. Before reusing, bring to boil then let cool.

❧　❧　❧

1 *Seque los filetes de pescado ligeramente; corte en pedazos grandes. Marine el pescado con la mezcla ① por 1 día.*

2 *Precaliente el horno a 500°F (260°C). Quítele el jugo al pescado; coloque el pescado en un recipiente de hornear cubierto con papel aluminio; hornee en la parrilla central hasta que esté cocido y dorado por ambos lados, como 12 minutos. Unte un poco de aceite de sésamo sobre el pescado. Para darle más sabor, rocíele jugo de limón cuando lo sirva.*

☐ *Salmón, bacalao, castañola, y roncador amarillo pueden sustituirse en esta receta. Los ingredientes que sobren de ① pueden guardarse para otros usos. Antes de volver a usarlos, haga hervir y deje enfriar.*

燻烤魚排　Baked-Smoked Fish Fillets

Filete de Pescado Horneado-Ahumado

4人份 · serves 4
4 porciones

魚肉 .... 450公克（12兩）

①
酒、糖 各1大匙
醬油 2½大匙
鹽 1小匙
蔥（拍扁）...................... 4支
薑（拍碎）...................... 4片

②
茶 .... ½杯
糖 2大匙

❧　❧　❧

①
1 lb. (450g) fish fillet

1 T.ea.: cooking wine,
　sugar
2½ T. soy sauce
1 t. salt
4 green onions, pressed
4 slices ginger root, mashed

②
½ c. tea
2 T. sugar

❧　❧　❧

①
1 lb. (450g) filete de pescado

1 C. c/u: vino para cocinar,
　azúcar
2½ C. salsa de soya
1 c. sal
4 cebollines, machacados
4 rebanadas raíz de jengibre,
　machacadas

②
½ tz. té
2 C. azúcar

1 魚肉切大塊加 **①** 料醃20分鐘。鐵架上塗少許油，魚置其上。

2 烤箱熱至500°F（260°C），將魚放入烤箱上層，烤盤內鋪鋁箔紙再置 **②** 料放於烤箱下層，大火烤約20分鐘，取出塗上麻油即可。

☐ 龍利魚、鯧魚、黃魚或其他肉質細嫩的魚均適合燻烤。

燻烤全魚 將魚由背部剖開成一大片，加 **①** 料醃6小時後，同法燻烤即可。

❧　❧　❧

1 Cut fish in large pieces; marinate in **①** for at least 20 minutes. Grease top rack of oven.

2 Preheat oven to 500°F (260°C). Bake the fish on top oven rack, and **②** on a baking pan lined with aluminum foil on a rack below, over high heat, until done, about 20 minutes. Remove and sprinkle with sesame oil.

☐ Flounder, pomfret, yellow croaker, or any tender fish is suitable for this recipe.

Baked-Smoked Whole Fish Cut from the back of the fish, then open to butterfly; marinate in **①** for 6 hours. Follow the above steps to make this dish.

❧　❧　❧

1 *Corte el pescado en pedazos grandes; marine en* **①** *por lo menos 20 minutos. Enmantequille la parrilla superior del horno.*

2 *Precaliente el horno a 500°F (260°C). Hornee el pescado encima de la parrilla superior, y* **②** *en un recipiente de hornear cubierto con papel de aluminio en la parrilla de abajo, a fuego alto, hasta que esté listo, como 20 minutos. Saque y rocíe con aceite de sésamo.*

☐ *Lenguado, castañola, roncador amarillo, o cualquier pescado tierno es apropiado para sustituir en esta receta.*

Pescado Entero Horneado-Ahumado *Corte por el dorso del pescado, luego ábralo en forma de mariposa; marine en* **①** *por 6 horas. Siga los procedimientos de arriba para preparar este platillo.*

燻烤全魚 · Baked-Smoked Whole Fish
Pescado Entero Horneado-Ahumado

14

鰻魚 1條
鐵針或竹籤（10-15公分長）3支

① 醬油 4大匙
酒 2大匙
糖 3大匙
鰹魚粉 .... ½小匙
水 .... ½杯

ಎ   ಎ   ಎ

1 eel
3 steel or wooden skewers
　4"-6"(10cm-15cm) long

① 4 T. soy sauce
2 T. cooking wine
3 T. sugar
½ t. dashi
½ c. water

ಎ   ಎ   ಎ

1 anguila
3 palillos de hierro o madera
　para brochetas de 4"-6"
　(10cm-15cm) de largo

① *4 C. salsa de soya*
2 C. vino para cocinar
3 C. azúcar
½ c. dashi
½ tz. agua

① 鰻魚取出中間大骨分切成兩段，用鐵針在頭、尾及中間穿過以免烤時反捲。① 料燒煮6分鐘至汁呈濃稠狀備用。

② 烤箱熱至500°F（260°C），魚放入烤箱中層烤約20分鐘（烤時需翻面）烤至兩面均乾後塗上 ① 料烤5分鐘，翻面再塗 ① 料續烤5分鐘即成。

ಎ   ಎ   ಎ

① Remove the backbone of the eel. Cut the eel in two sections. Thread the skewers lengthwise from the head to the tail. Thread the skewer through both halves at the center and at both ends of the eel to prevent curling during baking. Cook ① until liquid has thickened, 6 minutes; set aside.

② Preheat oven to 500°F (260°C). Bake the fish on the middle oven rack until both sides dry out (turn the fish over during baking), about 20 minutes. Spread cooked ① on one side of the fish and bake for 5 minutes. Turn the fish over; spread the remaining portion of ① on the other side of the fish and bake for another 5 minutes. Serve.

ಎ   ಎ   ಎ

① *Quítele la espina dorsal a la anguila. Corte la anguila en dos secciones. Inserte los palillos a lo largo, de la cabeza a la cola. Inserte un palillo por ambas mitades en el centro de ambos lados de la anguila para que no se enrosquen al hornear. Cocine ① hasta que el líquido se espese, 6 minutos; deje aparte.*

② *Precaliente el horno a 500°F (260°C). Hornee el pescado en la parrilla central del horno hasta que ambos lados se resequen (voltee el pescado una vez durante la cocción), como 20 minutos. Vacíe ① cocido sobre un lado del pescado y hornee por 5 minutos. Voltee el pescado; vacíele la porción restante de ① por el otro lado del pescado y hornee por otros 5 minutos. Sirva.*

沙茶淋魚　　Fish in Barbecue Sauce
Pescado en Salsa de Barbacoa

魚 .... 300公克（8兩）

①
鹽 .... ¼ 小匙
酒 .... 1 大匙

②
蔥、蒜末 各1大匙
薑末 .... 1 小匙

③
沙茶醬 .... 3 大匙
醬油 .... 1 大匙
糖 .... ½ 小匙
麻油 .... 1 小匙
水 .... ¼ 杯
太白粉 .... ½ 小匙

🍃　🍃　🍃

⅔ lb.(300g) fish

①
¼ t. salt
1 T. cooking wine

②
1 T. ea.(minced): green
　onions, garlic cloves
1 t. minced ginger root

③
3 T. barbecue (sa-tsa) sauce
1 T. soy sauce
½ t. sugar
1 t. sesame oil
¼ c. water
½ t. cornstarch

🍃　🍃　🍃

⅔ lb. (300g) pescado

①
¼ c. sal
1 C. vino para cocinar

②
1 C. c/u, (finamente picado):
　cebollín, diente de ajo
1 c. raíz de jengibre finamente
　picada

③
3 C. salsa de barbacoa (sa-tsa)
1 C. salsa de soya
½ c. azúcar
1 c. aceite de sésamo
¼ tz. agua
½ c. maicena

---

1 魚在肉厚處劃二、三刀，加 **①** 料醃10分鐘，水開以大火蒸約10分鐘（或微波爐加熱5分鐘）至熟取出，蒸汁倒掉。

2 油1大匙燒熱，炒香 **②** 料，隨入調勻的 **③** 料煮滾，淋於魚上即成。

☐ 可依喜好撒上香菜或蔥花。

🍃　🍃　🍃

1 Score fish in thick areas; marinate in **①** for 10 minutes. Bring water to boil; steam the fish over high heat until done, about 10 minutes (or microwave 5 minutes); remove. Discard the cooking juice.

2 Heat 1 T. oil; stir-fry **②** until fragrant. Stir in mixture **③** until boiling. Sprinkle over the fish; serve.

☐　Sprinkle with coriander or chopped green onion, if desired.

🍃　🍃　🍃

1 *Haga cortes en las áreas gruesas; marine en* **①** *por 10 minutos. Haga hervir agua; cocine el pescado al vapor sobre fuego alto hasta que se cueza, como 10 minutos (o en el horno microondas por 5 minutos); retire. Tire el jugo en que se coció.*

2 *Caliente 1 C. de aceite; fría-revolviendo* **②** *hasta que esté aromático. Agregue revolviendo la mezcla* **③** *hasta que hierva. Vacíe sobre el pescado; sirva.*

☐　*Espolvoree con cilantro o cebollín, si gusta.*

蔥油淋魚

Pescado en Jugo de Cebolla

Fish in Onion Juice

魚片（2公分厚）300公克（8兩）

① 鹽 .... ¼ 小匙
　酒 .... 1 大匙

② 蔥絲 .... ¼ 杯
　紅辣椒絲 .... 1 小匙
　胡椒 .... ⅛ 小匙

③ 酒 .... 1 大匙
　醬油 .... 2 大匙
　鹽、糖 .... 各⅓小匙
　高湯或水 .... 4 大匙

⅔ lb.(300g) fish fillet, ¾"
　(2cm) thick

① ¼ t. salt
　1 T. wine

② ¼ c. shredded green onions
　1 t. shredded red chili pepper
　⅛ t. pepper

③ 1 T. cooking wine
　2 T. soy sauce
　⅓ t. ea.: salt, sugar
　4 T. stock or water

⅔ lb. (300g) filete de pescado,
　¾" (2cm) de grueso

① ¼ c. sal
　1 C. vino

② ¼ tz. cebollines finamente
　　picados
　1 c. chile rojo picado
　⅛ c. pimienta

③ 1 C. vino para cocinar
　2 C. salsa de soya
　⅓ c. c/u: sal, azúcar
　4 C. caldo o agua

1 魚片加 ① 料醃10分鐘，水開以大火蒸約10分鐘至魚肉剛熟取出，湯汁倒掉，撒上 ② 料，再淋滾熱的油3大匙，③ 料煮滾淋於魚上，可依喜好加少許香菜。

☐ 這道菜的魚汁拌飯或拌熟麵線食用均佳。

清蒸龍利魚　龍利魚肉質細嫩適合清蒸，其它如石斑魚、鯧魚、黃魚等都可用來蒸、炸或燒，但蒸魚時尤需挑選新鮮的。

1 Marinate the fish in ① for 10 minutes. Bring water to boil; steam the fish over high heat until just done, about 10 minutes; remove; discard the cooking juice. Sprinkle on ② then 3 T. bubbling hot oil cooked with ③ over the fish. Serve with coriander, if desired.

☐ Fish juice from this dish mixed with cooked rice or thin noodles tastes great.

Steamed Flounder Since flounder's meat texture is tender, it's best for steaming. Other fish such as grouper, pomfret, and yellow croaker are all good for steaming, deep-frying, or cooking in sauce. However, opt for extra fresh fish for steaming.

1 *Marine el pescado en* ① *por 10 minutos. Haga hervir agua; cocine el pescado al vapor sobre fuego alto hasta que se cueza, como 10 minutos; retire; tire el jugo en que se coció. Espolvoree con* ② *luego vacíe 3 C. de aceite hirviendo cocinado con* ③ *, sobre el pescado. Sirva con cilantro, si gusta.*

☐ *El jugo de pescado de este platillo combinado con arroz cocido o fideos delgados sabe delicioso.*

Lenguado al Vapor *Ya que la textura de la carne de lenguado es tierna, es lo mejor para cocer al vapor. Otros pescados como mero, castañola, y roncador amarillo son buenos para cocer al vapor, freír con bastante aceite, o cocer en salsa. Sin embargo, para cocer al vapor use pescado bien fresco.*

清蒸龍利魚 · Steamed Flounder
Lenguado al Vapor

蠔油魚肉豆腐 Fish & Bean Curd in Oyster Sauce

Pescado y Tofu en Salsa de Ostiones

4人份・serves 4
4 porciones

魚肉	....	225公克（6兩）
豆腐（圖1）	....	1盒
蔥段（3公分長）	....	6段
燙熟青菜	....	225公克（6兩）

1
鹽 .... ¼小匙，酒 1小匙
太白粉 1大匙

2
鹽 .... ¼小匙，太白粉 ... 1大匙

3
蠔油、醬油 各1½大匙
糖、麻油 .... 各½小匙
水或高湯 .... ¾杯
太白粉 .... ½大匙

🐟　🐟　🐟

½ lb. (225g) fish fillet
⅔ lb. (300g) bean curd
(Fig.1)
6 green onion sections,
1¼" (3cm) long
½ lb. (225g) cooked green
leafy vegetable

1 ¼ t. salt, 1T. cornstarch
1t. cooking wine

2 ¼ t. salt, 1T. cornstarch

3 1½ T. ea.: oyster sauce,
soy sauce
½ t. ea.: sugar, sesame oil
¾ c. water or stock
½ T. cornstarch

🐟　🐟　🐟

½ lb. (225g) filete de pescado
⅔ lb. (300g) tofu (Fig. 1)
6 secciones de cebollín, 1¼"
(3cm) de largo
½ lb. (225g) hojas de vegetal
verde cocidas

1 ¼ c. sal, 1 C. maicena
1 c. vino para cocinar

2 ¼ c. sal, 1 C. maicena

3 1½ C. c/u: salsa de ostiones,
salsa de soya
½ c. c/u: azúcar, aceite de
sésamo
¾ tz. agua o caldo
½ C. maicena

1

1 魚肉切3公分×4公分×1公分薄片，加 **1** 料略醃。豆腐切與魚肉同大小之片狀，排於抹油盤上，撒 **2** 料上擺魚片，水開以大火蒸8分鐘，蒸汁倒出。

2 油1大匙燒熱，炒香蔥段，隨入調勻的 **3** 料拌勻煮滾，淋於魚上，燙熟青菜置旁即成。

☐ 蒸豆腐時，蓋子可稍留縫隙使透氣，以免豆腐變形或變粗糙。

🐟　🐟　🐟

1 Thinly slice fish into 1¼" × 1½" × ½" (3cm×4cm×1cm) pieces; marinate in **1** briefly. Slice the bean curd the same size as the fish slices. Arrange bean curd slices on a greased plate; sprinkle on **2**; top with fish slices. Bring water to boil; steam the mixture for 8 minutes over high heat. Discard the cooking juice.

2 Heat 1 T. oil; stir-fry green onions until fragrant. Stir in mixture **3** until boiling and combined. Sprinkle over the fish; arrange green vegetable on the side.

☐ When steaming bean curd, leave the lid slightly ajar to let steam escape so bean curd will not crumble and become tough.

🐟　🐟　🐟

1 *Corte el pescado en pedazos delgados de 1¼" × 1½" × ½" (3cm × 4cm × 1cm); marine en **1** brevemente. Corte el tofu del mismo tamaño como los pedazos de pescado. Acomode los pedazos de tofu en un plato enmantequillado; espolvoréele **2**; cubra con los pedazos de pescado. Haga hervir agua; cocine al vapor la mezcla por 8 minutos sobre fuego alto, luego tire el jugo en que se coció.*

2 *Caliente 1 C. de aceite; fría-revolviendo el cebollín hasta que esté aromático. Agregue revolviendo la mezcla **3** hasta que hierva y esté combinado. Vacíe sobre el pescado; acomódele el vegetal verde a un lado.*

☐ *Cuando cocine el tofu al vapor, deje la olla un poco destapada para dejar que escape el vapor y así el tofu no se desbatará ni se pondrá duro.*

香蒜蒸魚　Steamed Garlic-Flavored Fish

Pescado con Ajo al Vapor

虱目魚 .... 300公克（8兩）

① 鹽 .... ¼ 小匙
酒 .... 1 大匙

② 蒜末 .... 3 大匙
嫩薑絲 .... 2 大匙

③ 醬油膏 .... 1½ 大匙
麻油 .... 1 大匙

🐌　　🐌　　🐌

⅔ lb.(300g) milkfish

① ¼ t. salt
1 T. cooking wine

② 3 T. minced garlic cloves
2 T. shredded baby ginger root

③ 1½ T. soy sauce paste
1 T. sesame oil

🐌　　🐌　　🐌

⅔ lb. (300g) pez comestible

① ¼ c. sal
1 C. vino para cocinar

② 3 C. dientes de ajo finamente picado
2 C. raíz de jengibre pequeña rallada

③ 1½ C. pasta de salsa de soya
1 C. aceite de sésamo

① 魚在肉厚處劃一、二刀，調 ① 料後置盤，再加 ② 料，並淋上 ③ 料，水開以大火蒸約10分鐘即可。

☐ 醬油膏、嫩薑絲可分別用醬油、薑絲取代。

☐ 蒸魚時除用蒸籠或電鍋外，亦可用炒鍋或深鍋（鍋內置筷子或蒸盤，圖1、2）或使用微波爐也十分方便。

🐌　　🐌　　🐌

① Score the fish in thick areas; mix ① then place on a plate; add ② ; sprinkle on ③ . Bring water to boil; steam fish over high heat for 10 minutes.

☐ Soy sauce paste and shredded baby ginger root may be substituted for soy sauce and shredded ginger root.

☐ Stir-frying pan or deep pan (place chopsticks or a plate in the pan; see Figs. 1 & 2) can be substituted for steamer or electric cooker for steaming. Use a microwave as another convenient way for steaming.

🐌　　🐌　　🐌

① *Haga cortes en las áreas gruesas del pescado; mezcle* ① *luego coloque en un plato; agregue* ② ; *rocíele* ③ . *Haga hervir agua; cueza el pescado al vapor por 10 minutos.*

☐ *La pasta de salsa de soya y la raíz de jengibre pequeña pueden sustituirse por salsa de soya y raíz de jengibre rallada.*

☐ *Una sartén para freír-revolviendo o una sartén honda puede sustituirse por una olla vaporera u olla eléctrica para cocer al vapor (coloque palillos chinos o un plato en la sartén; vea Figs. 1 y 2). Use el microondas como otro método conveniente para cocer al vapor.*

1

2

Sábalo Americano al Vapor

鰣魚 .... 600公克（1斤）
絞肉 .... ½杯

① 酒 1大匙
   鹽 1小匙

② 香菇丁、蔥花 各2大匙
   蒜、薑末 .... 各½大匙
   辣椒（切片）.................... 1條

③ 醬油 1½大匙
   酒、麻油 各1大匙
   味精 .... 少許

🐟   🐟   🐟

1⅓ lbs. (600g) American shad
½ c. ground meat

① **1 T. cooking wine**
   1 t. salt

② **2 T. ea.(chopped): Chinese black mushrooms, green onions**
   ½ T. ea.(minced): garlic cloves, ginger root
   1 chili pepper, sliced

③ **1½ T. soy sauce**
   1 T. ea.: cooking wine, sesame oil

🐟   🐟   🐟

1⅓ lbs. (600g) sábalo americano
½ tz. carne molida

① *1 C. vino para cocinar*
   1 c. sal

② *2 C. c/u (picado): hongos negros chinos, cebollín*
   ½ C. c/u (finamente picado): dientes de ajo, raíz de jengibre
   1 chile rebanado

③ *1½ C. salsa de soya*
   1 C. c/u: vino para cocinar, aceite de sésamo

1 鰣魚去內臟（可不去鱗）洗淨，在肉厚處劃二、三刀，加 ① 料抹勻醃20分鐘後拭乾。

2 將絞肉、 ② 料及 ③ 料拌勻鋪在魚身上，水開大火蒸12分鐘至魚肉剛熟即可。

🐟   🐟   🐟

1 Remove the entrails (scaling is optional) then clean the fish. Make 2 to 3 cuts on the thick end. Marinate in ① for 20 minutes; pat dry.

2 Combine ground meat, ②, and ③; spread over the fish. Bring water to boil; steam the fish over high heat until just done, 12 minutes. Serve.

🐟   🐟   🐟

1 *Quite las entrañas (descamar es opcional) y luego limpie el pescado. Haga 2 ó 3 cortes en la orilla gruesa. Marine en ① por 20 minutos; seque ligeramente.*

2 *Combine la carne molida, ②, y ③; unte sobre el pescado. Haga hervir agua; cueza el pescado al vapor hasta que esté casi listo, 12 minutos. Sirva.*

鱈魚片(2公分厚)300公克(8兩)
雪菜（切碎）................. ½ 杯

① 酒 1大匙
鹽 .... ½ 小匙

② 肉絲 .... ⅓杯
太白粉、酒 各1小匙

③ 紅辣椒（切片）............... 1 條
蒜末 .... ½ 大匙

④ 醬油 .... ⅔大匙
麻油 1小匙
胡椒 .... 少許

❧　❧　❧

⅔ lb.(300g) cod fillet,
¾"(2cm) thick
½ c. salted rape greens
  chopped

① 1 T. cooking wine
½ t. salt

② ⅓ c. shredded meat
1 t. ea.: cornstarch,
  cooking wine

③ 1 red chili pepper, sliced
½ T. minced garlic cloves

④ ⅔ T. soy sauce
1 t. sesame oil
dash of pepper

❧　❧　❧

⅔ lb. (300g) filete de bacalao,
¾" (2cm) de grueso
½ tz. repollo escabechado,
  picado

① 1 C. vino para cocinar
½ c. sal

② ⅓ tz. carne desmenuzada
1 c. c/u: maicena, vino para
  cocinar

③ 1 chile rojo, rebanado
½ C. dientes de ajo finamente
  picado

④ ⅔ C. salsa de soya
1 c. aceite de sésamo
pizca de pimienta

雪菜蒸魚
Pescado con Repollo

Fish with Greens

1 鱈魚片加 **①** 料抹勻醃10分鐘。**②** 料拌勻備用。

2 油4大匙燒熱，將肉絲炒熟鏟出，餘油炒香 **③** 料，隨入雪菜略炒，再將肉絲倒回一同拌勻鋪在魚上，並淋上 **④** 料，水開大火蒸10分鐘至熟即成。

□ 雪菜亦可用鹹菜或花瓜取代。蒸魚宜選愈新鮮的魚愈佳，若使用冷藏過的魚較不易熟透，需延長蒸魚的時間。

❧　❧　❧

1 Marinate the fillet in **①** for 10 minutes. Mix **②** until blended; set aside.

2 Heat 4 T. oil; stir-fry shredded meat until done; remove. Stir-fry **③** with remaining oil until fragrant; add salted rape greens; stir lightly; return cooked meat to wok; mix well; pour mixture over the fish evenly; sprinkle **④** on top. Bring water to boil; steam the fish over high heat until done, 10 minutes. Serve.

□ Pickled mustard cabbage or pickled cucumber may be substituted for salted rape greens. The fresher the fish, the better for steaming. If frozen fish is used, increase steaming time to cook through.

❧　❧　❧

1 *Marine el filete en* **①** *por 10 minutos. Mezcle* **②** *hasta que se combine; deje aparte.*

2 *Caliente 4 C. de aceite; fría-revolviendo la carne desmenuzada hasta que esté lista; retire. Fría-revolviendo* **③** *con el aceite restante hasta que esté aromático; agregue el repollo escabechado; revuelva ligeramente; regrese la carne cocida a la sartén wok; mezcle bien; vacíe la mezcla sobre el pescado en forma pareja; rocíele* **④** *encima. Haga hervir agua; cueza el pescado a fuego alto hasta que esté listo, 10 minutos. Sirva.*

□ *Repollo o pepino escabechado puede sustituirse por nabos verdes salados. Mientras más fresco esté el pescado mejor se cocerá al vapor. Si usa pescado congelado, aumente el tiempo de cocción al vapor para que se cueza completamente.*

豆醬蒸魚　　Fish with Bean Sauce

Pescado con Salsa de Frijol de Soya

4 porciones

魚片（2公分厚）300公克（8兩）

① 鹽 .... ¼小匙
　 酒 1大匙

② 黃豆醬 2大匙
　 或味噌 2大匙
　 醬油 .... ½大匙
　 味精 .... 隨意

③ 薑絲 2大匙
　 紅辣椒絲 1大匙

❧　　❧　　❧

⅔ lb.(300g) fish fillet,
¾ " (2cm) thick

① ¼ t. salt
　 1 T. cooking wine

② 2 T. fermented soy bean
　　 sauce or 2 T. miso
　 ½ T. soy sauce

③ 2 T. shredded ginger root
　 1 T. shredded red chili
　　 pepper

❧　　❧　　❧

⅔ lb. (300g) filete de pescado,
¾" (2cm) de grueso

① ¼ c. sal
　 1 C. vino para cocinar

② 2 C. salsa de frijol de soya
　　 fermentada ó 2 C. miso
　 ½ C. salsa de soya

③ 2 C. raíz de jengibre rallada
　 1 C. chile rojo picado

1️⃣ 魚片抹上 ① 料醃10分鐘。

2️⃣ 將魚置蒸盤上，均勻的擺上 ② 料，並撒 ③ 料，水開以大火蒸約10分鐘即可。

☐ 黃豆醬可視鹹度增減份量。金線魚（圖1）也適合做豆醬蒸魚。

❧　　❧　　❧

1️⃣ Marinate the fillet in ① for 10 minutes.

2️⃣ Place the fillet in a heatproof bowl; spread on ② evenly; sprinkle with
③. Bring water to boil; steam the fillet over high heat for 10 minutes; serve.

☐ Adjust the amount of fermented soy bean sauce to taste. Golden-thread
fish (Fig. 1) may be used for this dish.

❧　　❧　　❧

1️⃣ *Marine el filete en ① por 10 minutos.*

2️⃣ *Coloque el filete en un tazón para hornear; úntele ② en forma pareja;
espolvoree con ③. Haga hervir agua; cueza el filete al vapor a fuego alto
por 10 minutos; sirva.*

☐ *Ajuste la cantidad de la salsa de frijol de soya fermentada al gusto. Se
puede usar el pescado de (Fig. 1) para este platillo.*

1

Pescado y Jugo de Limón

魚.....................450公克（12兩）
香菜葉...........................2大匙

① 鹽..................................½小匙
　酒...................................1大匙

② 檸檬汁、醬油............各1½大匙
　蒜末、紅辣椒末、香菜莖末.......
　.......................................各1大匙
　糖、味精....................各½小匙
　高湯....................................¼杯

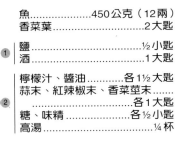

1 lb. (450g) fish
2 T. coriander leaves

① ½ t. salt
1T. cooking wine

② 1½ T. ea.: lemon juice, soy
　　sauce
1T. ea. (minced):garlic
　　cloves, red chili pepper,
　　coriander stems
½ t. sugar
¼ c. stock

1 lb. (450g) pescado
2 C. hojas de cilantro

① ½ c. sal
1 C. vino para cocinar

② 1½ C. c/u: jugo de limón, salsa
　　de soya
1 C. c/u (finamente picado):
　　dientes de ajo, chile, tallos
　　de cilantro
½ c. azúcar
¼ tz. caldo

1 魚調 ① 料醃10分鐘， ② 料調勻備用。

2 水燒開，將魚蒸約10分鐘（或以微波爐加熱5分鐘）至熟，取出淋上 ② 料並撒上香菜葉即可。

□ 蒸魚要領：蒸魚需用大火，水開後才放入魚，至魚肉剛熟即可，蒸魚時間控制得當，魚肉滑嫩而鮮美。通常1斤（600公克）的魚蒸約12分鐘，時間過久口感較澀。

1 Marinate the fish in ① for 10 minutes. Mix ② evenly; set aside.

2 Bring water to boil; steam fish until done, about 10 minutes (or microwave 5 minutes); remove. Drizzle with ② and sprinkle with coriander leaves; serve.

□ Tips for steaming fish: Bring water to boil then steam the fish over high heat. Remove the fish when just done. If the steaming time is controlled properly, the fish is tender and tasty. For fish that weigh 1⅓ lbs. (600g), steam about 12 minutes to get best results. Overcooking will make the fish tough.

1 *Marine el pescado en* ① *por 10 minutos. Mezcle* ② *completamente; deje aparte.*

2 *Haga hervir agua; cocine el pescado al vapor hasta que esté listo; como 10 minutos (o en el microondas por 5 minutos); retire. Rocíe con* ② *y espolvoree con las hojas de cilantro; sirva.*

□ *Sugerencias para cocer pescado al vapor: Haga hervir agua, luego cueza el pescado al vapor a fuego alto. Saque el pescado cuando esté casi listo. Si el tiempo de cocer al vapor se controla adecuadamente, el pescado estará tierno y sabroso. Para pescado que pese 1⅓ lbs.(600g), cueza al vapor como 12 minutos para obtener los mejores resultados. Si el pescado se cocina demasiado, quedará duro.*

豆豉蒸魚　Fish & Black Beans

Pescado y Frijoles Negros

魚	600公克（1斤）	
絞肉	75公克（2兩）	
嫩薑絲	2大匙	

①
酒	1大匙
鹽	½小匙

②
豆豉	1½大匙
蒜末	½大匙
辣椒（切片）	1條

③
醬油	2½大匙
酒	1大匙
麻油	1小匙
味精	少許

ぉ　ぉ　ぉ

1⅓ lbs. (600g) fish
2½ oz. (75g) ground meat
2 T. shredded baby ginger root

①
1 T. cooking wine
½ t. salt

②
1½ T. fermented black beans
½ T. minced garlic cloves
1 chili pepper, sliced

③
2½ T. soy sauce
1 T. cooking wine
1 t. sesame oil

ぉ　ぉ　ぉ

1⅓ lbs. (600g) pescado
2½ oz. (75g) carne molida
2 C. raíz de jengibre pequeña rallada

①
1 C. vino para cocinar
½ c. sal

②
1½ C. frijoles negros fermentados
½ C. dientes de ajo finamente picados
1 chile rebanado

③
2½ C. salsa de soya
1 C. vino para cocinar
1 c. aceite de sésamo

① 魚在肉厚處劃刀痕，加 **①** 料拌勻醃20分鐘。

② 油1大匙燒熱，炒香 **②** 料，隨入絞肉炒熟，續入 **③** 料略炒後鏟出鋪在魚身上。水開大火蒸12分鐘至魚肉熟即可，食時撒上嫩薑絲則味更佳。

ぉ　ぉ　ぉ

① Score fish in thick areas; marinate in **①** for 20 minutes.

② Heat 1 T. oil; stir-fry **②** until fragrant; cook and stir ground meat until done; stir in **③** briefly; remove; spread over the fish. Bring water to boil; steam the fish over high heat until cooked through, 12 minutes. For extra flavor, sprinkle on shredded ginger root before serving.

ぉ　ぉ　ぉ

① *Haga cortes en las áreas gruesas del pescado; marine en* **①** *por 20 minutos.*

② *Caliente 1 C. de aceite; fría-revolviendo* **②** *hasta que esté aromático; cocine y revuelva la carne molida hasta que esté lista; agregue revolviendo* **③** *brevemente; retire; unte sobre el pescado. Haga hervir agua; cueza el pescado al vapor a fuego alto hasta que esté completamente cocido, 12 minutos. Para mayor sabor, espolvoree raíz de jengibre rallada antes de servir.*

豉汁蒸魚頭　Fish Head & Black Beans

Cabeza de Pescado y Frijoles Negros 4人份 · serves 4
4 porciones

魚頭 .... 600公克（1斤）

豆豉（切碎）、蒜末 各1大匙
薑末 2大匙
辣椒（切片） 1條
醬油、酒 各1½大匙
麻油、太白粉 各1大匙
鹽 .... ½小匙
糖 .... ¼小匙
胡椒 .... 少許

❧　　❧　　❧

1⅓ lbs. (600g) fish head

1 T. ea.: chopped
　fermented black beans,
　minced garlic cloves
2 T. minced ginger root
1 chili pepper, sliced
1½ T. ea.: soy sauce,
　cooking wine
1 T. ea.: sesame oil,
　cornstarch
½ t. salt
¼ t. sugar
dash of pepper

❧　　❧　　❧

1⅓ lbs. (600g) cabeza de
　pescado

1 C. c/u: frijoles negros
　fermentados machacados,
　dientes de ajo finamente
　picados
2 C. raíz de jengibre finamente
　picada
1 chile rebanado
1½ C. c/u: salsa de soya, vino
　para cocinar
1 C. c/u: aceite de sésamo,
　maicena
½ c. sal
¼ c. azúcar
pizca de pimienta

▇1 魚頭切大塊（圖1），加 ❶ 料醃30分鐘。水開用大火蒸15分鐘即可趁熱食用。

□ 石斑魚、鰱魚、鯛魚、馬頭魚、草魚及鮭魚頭都適合做豉汁蒸魚頭或紅燒魚頭，選較大的魚頭較佳。

❧　　❧　　❧

▇1 Cut fish head into large pieces (Fig. 1); marinate in ❶ for 30 minutes. Bring water to boil; steam fish head over high heat for 15 minutes; serve hot.

□ Head of a grouper, silver carp, hagfish, horsehead, grass carp, or salmon is suitable for this dish or for cooking in soy sauce. The larger the fish head, the better for this recipe.

❧　　❧　　❧

▇1 *Corte la cabeza de pescado en pedazos grandes (Fig. 1); marine en ❶ por 30 minutos. Haga hervir agua; cueza la cabeza de pescado al vapor a fuego alto por 15 minutos; sirva caliente.*

□ *Cabeza de mero, carpa dorada, lamprea glutinosa, carpa, o salmón es adecuada para este platillo o para cocinar en salsa de soya. Mientras más grande sea la cabeza será mejor para esta receta.*

1

麒麟蒸魚　Auspicious Steamed Fish
Pescado Afortunado al Vapor

魚 .... 600公克（1斤）
芥蘭菜（12公分長）....... 12棵
蔥絲 4大匙

1　酒 .... 1大匙，鹽 .... ½小匙

2　火腿、香菇、筍 各12片

3
高湯（連蒸魚汁）........... ¾杯
太白粉 .... ½大匙
酒 .... 1小匙，鹽 .... ½小匙
胡椒、味精 .... 各少許

🦐　🦐　🦐

1⅓ lbs. (600g) fish
12 bunches Chinese
　broccoli, 6"(12cm) long
4 T. shredded green onions

1　1 T. cooking wine, ½ t. salt

2　12 slices ea.: ham, Chinese
　black mushrooms,
　bamboo shoots

3
¾ c. stock (include liquid
　from steaming fish)
½ T. cornstarch
1 t. cooking wine, ½ t. salt
dash of pepper

🦐　🦐　🦐

1⅓ lbs. (600g) pescado
12 florecillas bróculi chino, 6"
(12cm) de lago
4 C. cebollines en tiras

1　*1 C. vino para cocinar, ½ c. sal*

2　*12 rebanadas c/u: jamón,*
　hongos negros chinos,
　brotes de bambú

3
¾ tz. caldo (incluye el líquido
　en que se coció el pescado al
　vapor)
½ C. maicena
1 c. vino para cocinar, ½ c. sal
pizca de pimienta

1　魚先切下頭、尾。魚身取肉（見第8頁），切成12片。將魚頭、尾及魚肉加 1 料略醃。魚肉拌入太白粉 ½ 大匙。

2　材料依圖順序排盤，水開大火蒸8分鐘至魚肉熟取出，並以炒熟之芥蘭菜圍邊，蔥絲擺中間，3 料煮開淋在魚上即可。火腿味鹹，加糖蒸約30分鐘後切薄片使用。

火腿蒸魚　做法同上，將整條魚上排 2 料蒸熟即可。

🦐　🦐　🦐

1　Cut off the head and tail of the fish. Fillet (see p.8) into 12 slices. Marinate the fillet slices, head, and tail in 1 briefly. Coat the fillet slices with ½ T. cornstarch.

2　Follow the picture to arrange the ingredients on a plate. Steam the fish over boiling water, over high heat until done, 8 minutes; remove. Arrange stir-fried Chinese broccoli around the fish. Arrange the shredded green onions lengthwise over the fish. Bring 3 to boil then pour it over the fish; serve. To reduce the salty taste add sugar to the ham; steam 30 minutes; slice thinly before using.

Ham Over Whole Fish Follow the same procedures as above, except arrange 2 on top of the whole fish without cutting the fish into pieces.

🦐　🦐　🦐

1　*Corte la cabeza y cola al pescado. Corte 12 filetes (vea p.8). Marine los filetes de pescado, la cabeza, y la cola en 1 brevemente. Reboce los pedazos de pescado con ½ C. maicena.*

2　*Vea la foto para acomodar los ingredientes en un plato. Cueza el pescado al vapor sobre agua hirviendo, a fuego alto hasta que esté listo, 8 minutos; retire. Acomode alrededor del pescado el bróculi chino que se frió-revolviendo. Acomode las tiras de cebollines a lo largo sobre el pescado. Haga hervir 3, luego vacíe sobre el pescado; sirva. Para reducir el sabor salado agregue azúcar al jamón; cueza al vapor por 30 minutos; corte en rebanadas delgadas antes de usar.*

Jamón Sobre Pescado Entero *Siga los mismos procedimientos de arriba, pero acomode 2 sobre el pescado entero, no lo corte en pedazos.*

火腿蒸魚・Ham Over Whole Fish
Jamón Sobre Pescado Entero

乾炸龍利魚
Deep-Fried Flounder

Lenguado Frito

龍利魚 .... 600公克（1斤）
「炸油」 .... 適量
蔥花 1½大匙

① 酒 1大匙
　 鹽 .... ½小匙

② 酒、高湯（或水）... 各1½大匙
　 醬油 .... ¾大匙

🐟　🐟　🐟

1⅓ lbs. (600g) flounder or
　　sole
oil for deep-frying
1½ T. chopped green
　　onions

① 1 T. cooking wine
　 ½ t. salt

② 1½ T. ea.: cooking wine,
　　stock or water
　 ¾ T. soy sauce

🐟　🐟　🐟

*1⅓ lbs. (600g) lenguado o
　　rodaballo
aceite para freír
1½ C. cebollín picado*

① *1 C. vino para cocinar
　 ½ c. sal*

② *1½ C. c/u: vino para cocinar,
　　caldo o agua
　 ¾ C. salsa de soya*

1️⃣　魚在肉厚處劃刀痕，加入 ① 料醃20分鐘，炸前拭乾。

2️⃣　「炸油」燒熱，放入魚大火炸約8分鐘至金黃色，皮肉均酥脆時撈出置盤。

3️⃣　油1大匙燒熱，先炒香蔥花，隨入 ② 料燒開後均勻地澆在魚上即成。

乾炸魚　用其他種類的魚取代龍利魚，其他材料及做法同上。

🐟　🐟　🐟

1️⃣　Score the fish in thick areas; marinate in ① for 20 minutes; remove and pat dry before deep-frying.

2️⃣　Heat oil for deep-frying. Deep-fry fish over high heat until golden and crispy all over, about 8 minutes; remove and place on a serving plate.

3️⃣　Heat 1 T. oil; stir-fry green onions until fragrant; stir in ② ; bring to boil then sprinkle over the fish.

Deep-Fried Fish Use other kinds of fish for flounder, other ingredients and procedures are the same as above.

🐟　🐟　🐟

1️⃣　*Haga cortes en las áreas gruesas del pescado; marine en* ① *por 20 minutos; retire y seque ligeramente antes de freír.*

2️⃣　*Caliente bastante aceite para freír. Fría el pescado a fuego alto hasta que esté todo dorado y crujiente, como 8 minutos; retire y coloque sobre el plato a servir.*

3️⃣　*Caliente 1 C. de aceite; fría-revolviendo el cebollín hasta que esté aromático; agregue revolviendo* ② *; haga herviry luego rocíe sobre el pescado.*

Pescado Frito Use otros tipos de pescado en lugar del lenguado, los ingredientes y procedimientos son como los de esta receta.

乾炸魚 · Deep Fried Fish
Pescado Frito

芝麻魚塊　**Sesame-Flavored Fried Fish**

Pescado Frito Sabor a Sésamo

魚肉 .... 300公克（8兩）
蛋黃 1個
「炸油」 ....適量

①
鹽 ....⅓小匙
糖 ....¼小匙
太白粉 1大匙

②
芝麻 3大匙
麵粉 2大匙

🐟　🐟　🐟

⅔ lb.(300g) spear fish or
　shark fillet
1 egg yolk
oil for deep-frying

①
⅓ t. salt
¼ t. sugar
1 T. cornstarch

②
3 T. sesame seeds
2 T. all-purpose flour

🐟　🐟　🐟

⅔ lb. (300g) pez vela o filete de
　tiburón
1 yema de huevo
aceite para freír

①
⅓ c. sal
¼ c. azúcar
1 C. maicena

②
3 C. semilla de sésamo
2 C. harina

1 魚肉切4公分×4公分×1公分之魚塊，加 **①** 料醃10分鐘。蛋黃打散，**②** 料拌勻，將魚塊先裹蛋黃再沾 **②** 料備炸。

2 「炸油」燒至八分熱，入魚塊以中火炸約3分鐘至金黃色並熟，即可取出。

☐ 油炸要領z ：炸油溫度保持在八分熱，350°F（180°C）左右效果最好，材料剛入鍋時油溫會下降，可使用大火，等溫度回升再改用中火炸。

🐟　🐟　🐟

1 Cut fish fillets into 1½" × 1½" × ½" (4cm × 4cm × 1cm) pieces. Marinate in **①** for 10 minutes. Beat egg yolk. Mix **②** evenly in a bowl. Coat the fillet pieces with beaten egg yolk first then **②** before frying.

2 Heat oil to medium-high. Deep-fry fish over medium heat until done and golden, about 3 minutes; remove.

☐ Deep-Frying Tip: For best results, maintain the frying oil temperature at medium-high (350°F or 180°C). When the fish first contact the hot oil, the oil temperature drops. Increase heat to high until oil temperature is brought up. Lower the heat to medium; continue frying process.

🐟　🐟　🐟

1 *Corte los filetes del pescado en pedazos de 1½" × 1½" × ½" (4cm × 4cm × 1cm). Marine en* **①** *por 10 minutos. Bata la yema. Mezcle* **②** *completamente en un tazón. Cubra los filetes con la yema luego cúbralos con* **②** *antes de freír.*

2 *Caliente bastante aceite a fuego moderado-alto. Fría el pescado a fuego moderado-alto hasta que esté listo y dorado, como 3 minutos; retire.*

☐ *Sugerencia para freír en bastante aceite: Para mejores resultados, mantenga la temperatura del aceite a moderado-alto (350°F ó 180°C). Cuando el pescado se pone en contacto con el aceite caliente por primera vez, la temperatura del aceite baja. Aumente el fuego a alto hasta que la temperatura suba. Baje el fuego a mediano; continúe con el procedimiento de freír.*

吉利魚排

Deep-Fried Fish Fillets

Filetes de Pescado Fritos

4人份 · serves 4
4 porciones

魚肉 .... 300公克（8兩）
「炸油」 3杯

① 鹽 .... ⅓小匙
酒 1大匙
胡椒 .... 少許

② 麵粉 3大匙
雞蛋（打散） 1個
麵包粉 .... ½杯

❧　　❧　　❧

⅔ lb.(300g) fish fillets
3 c. oil for deep-frying

① ⅓ t. salt
1 T. cooking wine
dash of pepper

② 3 T. all-purpose flour
1 egg, beaten
½ c. fine bread crumbs

❧　　❧　　❧

⅔ lb. (300g) filete de pescado
3 tz. aceite para freír

① ⅓ c. sal
1 C. vino para cocinar
pizca de pimienta

② 3 C. harina
1 huevo, batido
½ tz. pan desmenuzado

1 魚肉切1公分厚之大厚片，加❶ 料醃10分鐘，❷ 料分別盛在盤上，將魚肉依序裹上麵粉、蛋液、麵包粉備炸。

2 「炸油」燒熱，放入魚片以中火炸約2分鐘至金黃色並熟，取出切塊置盤即可。

☐ 油炸要領x ：炸油的量一般為材料的2倍以上，較能控制油溫及保持油炸效果。

❧　　❧　　❧

1 Cut fish fillets into ½" (1cm) thick slices; marinate in ❶ for 10 minutes. Place each ingredient in ❷ on separate plates. Coat fish with flour first, then beaten egg mixture, then bread crumbs for deep-frying.

2 Heat oil for deep-frying. Deep-fry fish over medium heat until done and golden, about 2 minutes. Remove; cut into pieces; place on a plate. Serve.

☐ Deep-frying Tip: For best results, the amount of frying oil should be more than double the amount of the ingredients in the pan to be fried to better control the frying temperature.

❧　　❧　　❧

1 *Corte los filetes de pescado en pedazos gruesos de ½" (1cm); Marine en ❶ por 10 minutos. Ponga cada ingrediente de ❷ en platos diferentes. Reboce el pescado con harina primero, luego con el huevo batido, luego con el pan desmoronado para freírlo.*

2 *Caliente bastante aceite para freír. Fría el pescado sobre fuego mediano hasta que esté listo y dorado, como 2 minutos. Retire; corte en pedazos; coloque en un plato. Sirva.*

☐ *Sugerencia para freír: Para mejores resultados, la cantidad del aceite para freír debe ser más del doble de los ingredientes en la sartén para poder controlar mejor la temperatura.*

五香鯧魚　Five-Spice Pomfret
Castañola con Cinco Especias

鯧魚（取中段）　300公克（8兩）
蛋黃 1個
地瓜粉或太白粉 3大匙
「炸油」 .... 適量

① 酒 1大匙
五香粉、鹽 .... 各¼小匙
糖、醬油 .... 各½大匙
蒜末 1大匙

ஃ　　ஃ　　ஃ

⅔ lb.(300g) pomfret, middle sections
1 egg yolk
3 T. sweet potato flour or cornstarch
oil for deep-frying

① **1 T. cooking wine**
¼ t. ea.: five-spice powder, salt
½ t. ea.: sugar, soy sauce
1 T. minced garlic cloves

ஃ　　ஃ　　ஃ

⅔ lb. (300g) castañola, las secciones centrales
1 yema de huevo
3 C. harina de camote o maicena
aceite para freír

① *1 C. vino para cocinar*
¼ c. c/u: polvo cinco especias, sal
½ c. c/u: azúcar, salsa de soya
1 C. ajo machacado

1 魚切約1.5公分厚片，加 ① 料醃15分鐘，炸前瀝乾，加蛋黃拌勻，再沾上太白粉備炸。

2 「炸油」燒至九分熱，入魚以中火炸約4分鐘至熟，並呈金黃色撈出即成。

☐ 可依喜好撒上胡椒鹽食用。魚肉沾太白粉後置約3分鐘（圖1）再油炸，可避免太白粉掉落太多。

ஃ　　ஃ　　ஃ

1 Cut fish into ⅝" (1.5cm) thick pieces; marinate in ① for 15 minutes; pat dry before frying. Mix in egg yolk evenly; coat with cornstarch.

2 Heat oil to high for deep-frying. Deep-fry fish over medium heat until done and golden, about 4 minutes; remove.

☐ Serve with pepper-salt, if desired. Let the cornstarch coated fish stand about 3 minutes (Fig. 1) before frying to prevent cornstarch from falling off too much during cooking.

ஃ　　ஃ　　ஃ

1 *Corte el pescado en pedazos gruesos de ⅝" (1.5cm); marine en ① por 15 minutos; seque ligeramente antes de freír. Mezcle en la yema de huevo completamente; reboce con maicena.*

2 *Caliente bastante aceite para freír. Fría el pescado a fuego moderado-alto hasta que esté listo y dorado, como 4 minutos; retire.*

☐ *Sirva con sal de grano de pimienta, si gusta. Después que lo haya rebozado con maicena deje reposar el pescado como 3 minutos (Fig. 1) antes de freír para que no se le caiga mucha maicena al cocinar.*

1

脆皮魚肚　　　　　　　　**Crispy Fish Bellies**

Pancitas de Pescado Crujientes

虱目魚肚或鮭魚肚300公克(8兩)
蛋黃 1個
地瓜粉或太白粉 3大匙
胡椒鹽 .... 隨意
「炸油」 .... 適量

① 鹽 .... ⅓小匙
　 酒 1小匙

⅔ lb.(300g) milkfish or
　salmon, belly parts
1 egg yolk
3 T. sweet potato flour or
　cornstarch
pepper-salt as desired
oil for deep-frying

① ⅓ t. salt
　1 t. cooking wine

⅔ lb. (300g) pez comestible o
　salmón, la parte de la
　barriga
1 yema de huevo
3 C. harina de camote o
　maicena
sal de grano de pimienta al
　gusto
aceite para freír

① ⅓ c. sal
　1 c. vino para cocinar

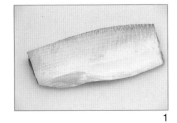

1

4人份 · serves 4
4 porciones

1 虱目魚肚加 ① 料醃10分鐘後瀝乾，拌入蛋黃再均勻的沾上地瓜粉備用。

2 「炸油」燒熱，將魚以中火炸約3分鐘至兩面呈金黃色並熟，沾胡椒鹽食之。

☐ 為免回鍋餘油太多不易處理，亦可將油量減為1½杯，將魚分次炸熟。

☐ 魚肚可改用煎的，以選用虱目魚肚（圖1）最佳，亦可用草魚肚等替代。

1 Marinate milkfish bellies in ① for 10 minutes; drain; mix in egg yolk evenly; coat all over with sweet potato flour; set aside.

2 Heat oil for deep-frying; deep-fry bellies over medium heat until done and golden on both sides, about 3 minutes; serve with pepper-salt as a dip.

☐ To avoid having too much frying oil left over, reduce oil to 1½ c.; deep-fry bellies a few at a time.

☐ You may pan-fry the fish bellies instead of deep-frying. Opt for milkfish bellies (Fig. 1) for this recipe. Grass carp bellies also work well.

1 *Marine las pancitas de pez comestible en* ① *por 10 minutos; escurra, mezcle en la yema de huevo totalmente; cubra completamente con la harina de camote; deje aparte.*

2 *Caliente bastante aceite para freír; fría las pancitas a fuego moderado-alto hasta que estén listas y doradas por ambos lados, como 3 minutos; sirva con sal pimienta como dip.*

☐ *Para que no le quede mucho aceite después de freír; reduzca el aceite a 1½ tz.; fría pocas pancitas cada vez.*

☐ *Puede sofreír las pancitas de pescado en vez de freír en bastante aceite. Opte por pancitas de pez comestible (Fig. 1) para esta receta. Pancitas de carpa también son adecuadas para esta receta.*

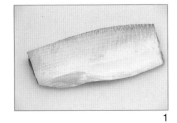

1

31

炸小魚　Deep-Fried Small Fish

Pescado Pequeño Frito

4人份 · serves 4
4 porciones

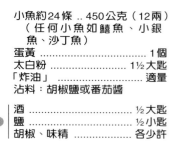

小魚約24條 .. 450公克（12兩）
（任何小魚如鱚魚、小銀
魚、沙丁魚）
蛋黃 1個
太白粉 .... 1½ 大匙
「炸油」 .... 適量
沾料：胡椒鹽或番茄醬

① 酒 .... ½ 大匙
鹽 .... ½ 小匙
胡椒、味精 .... 各少許

❧　　❧　　❧

24 small fish (smelt,
　grunion, sardine, etc.),
　1 lb. (450g)
1 egg yolk
1½ T. cornstarch
oil for deep-frying
dipping sauce: pepper-salt
　or ketchup

① ½ T. cooking wine
½ t. salt
dash of pepper

❧　　❧　　❧

24 pescados pequeños
　(esperingue, lisa, sardina,
　etc) 1 lb. (450g)
1 yema de huevo
1½ C. maicena
aceite para freír
salsa para dip: sal de grano de
　pimienta o catsup

① ½ C. vino para cocinar
½ c. sal
pizca de pimienta

1 小魚調 ① 料略醃後拭乾，拌上蛋黃及太白粉。「炸油」燒熱，入魚炸約4分鐘呈金黃色撈起，食時沾胡椒鹽或番茄醬。

□ 此種炸法炸出的魚肉較酥脆，冷吃熱食均宜，但魚會縮小外觀較差。

炸帶魚　帶魚去內臟並刮除表面銀質洗淨，在兩面劃刀痕後參照炸小魚，同法炸熟即可。

❧　　❧　　❧

1 Marinate small fish in ① briefly; pat dry; mix with egg yolk and cornstarch. Heat oil for deep-frying; deep-fry fish until golden, about 4 minutes; remove; serve with pepper-salt or ketchup.

□ This kind of deep-fried fish is crispier. It may be served hot or cold. However, the fish will shrink during frying and as a result, may not look very pretty when done.

Deep-Fried Ribbonfish Scale the fish; remove entrails; scrape off clear coating from skin; rinse; score on both sides. Follow the above procedure to deep-fry the ribbonfish.

❧　　❧　　❧

1 Marine los pescados pequeños en ① brevemente; seque ligeramente; mezcle con la yema de huevo y maicena. Caliente suficiente aceite para freír; fría los pescados hasta que estén dorados, como 4 minutos; retire; sirva con sal pimienta o catsup.

□ Este tipo de pescado frito es más crujiente. Se puede servir caliente o frío. Sin embargo, el pescado encogerá cuando se fría y como resultado no se verá muy bonito cuando esté listo.

Anguileta de Mar Frita Descame el pescado; quítele las entrañas; raspe y quite la capa clara de la piel; enjuague; haga cortes en ambos lados. Siga los procedimientos de arriba para freír la anguileta de mar.

炸帶魚 · Deep Fried Ribbonfish
Anguileta de Mar Frita

酥炸小魚　　Crispy Fish in Batter

Pescado Crujiente en Batido

4人份 · serves 4
4 porciones

小魚約24條 .. 450公克（12兩）
　（任何小魚如鱵魚、小銀魚、
　　沙丁魚）
「炸油」 .... 適量
沾料：番茄醬或胡椒鹽

① 酒 .... ½ 大匙
　 鹽 .... ½ 小匙
　 胡椒、味精 .... 各少許

② 水 .... ¾ 杯
　 糖 .... ½ 大匙
　 發粉 .... ½ 小匙
　 低筋麵粉 .... 1 杯
　 芝麻、沙拉油 各1大匙

🍃　　🍃　　🍃

24 small fish (smelt,
　　grunion, sardine, etc.),
　　1 lb. (450g)
oil for deep-frying
dipping sauce: ketchup or
　　pepper-salt

① ½ T. cooking wine
　 ½ t. salt
　 dash of pepper

② ¾ c. water
　 ½ T. sugar
　 ½ t. baking powder
　 1 c. low-gluten flour
　 1 T. ea.: sesame seeds, oil

🍃　　🍃　　🍃

24 pescados pequeños
　　(esperingue, lisa, sardina,
　　etc), 1 lb. (450g)
aceite para freír
salsa para dip: catsup o sal de
　　grano de pimienta

① ½ C. vino para cocinar
　 ½ c. sal
　 pizca de pimienta

② ¾ tz. agua
　 ½ C. azúcar
　 ½ c. polvo de hornear
　 1 tz. harina baja en gluten
　 1 C. c/u: semilla de sésamo,
　　　aceite

1 小魚加 ① 料略醃（若用活小魚，先川燙10秒再拌 ① 料）。② 料拌勻成麵糊備用。

2 「炸油」燒熱，魚拭乾沾裹上麵糊，入鍋炸約4分鐘至金黃色皮酥脆即可，食時沾番茄醬或胡椒鹽。

☐ 沾麵糊後炸出來的魚外表酥脆膨鬆宜趁熱食用，待涼變軟味道就差了。

🍃　　🍃　　🍃

1 Marinate small fish in ① briefly. (If live small fish are used, blanch fish 10 seconds then marinate in ①); mix ② to make flour batter.

2 Heat oil for deep-frying. Pat the fish dry; coat with paste; deep-fry until golden and crunchy, about 4 minutes. Serve with pepper-salt or ketchup.

☐ Fish coated with flour paste before deep-frying come out crispy. It's best to serve hot.

🍃　　🍃　　🍃

1 Marine los pescados pequeños en ① brevemente. (Si usa pescado pequeño vivo, sumérjalo en agua hirviendo por 10 segundos luego marine en ①); mezcle ② para preparar el batido de harina.

2 Caliente bastante aceite para freír. Seque el pescado ligeramente; cubra con la pasta; fría hasta que esté dorado y crujiente, como 4 minutos. Sirva con sal pimienta o catsup.

☐ Pescado cubierto con pasta de harina antes de freír sale crujiente. Es mejor servirlo caliente.

醋浸魚　　　　　Fish with Vinegar Sauce
Pescado con Salsa de Vinagre

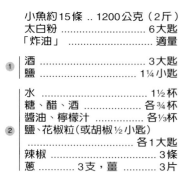

小魚約15條 .. 1200公克（2斤）
太白粉 6大匙
「炸油」 .... 適量

① | 酒 3大匙
   | 鹽 1¼小匙

② | 水 1½杯
   | 糖、醋、酒 .... 各¾杯
   | 醬油、檸檬汁 .... 各⅓杯
   | 鹽、花椒粒（或胡椒½小匙）
   | 各1大匙
   | 辣椒 3條
   | 蔥 .... 3支，薑 3片

🐟　　🐟　　🐟

15 small fish, 2⅔ lbs.
　(1200g)
6 T. cornstarch
oil for deep-frying

① | 3 T. cooking wine
   | 1¼ t. salt

② | 1½ c. water
   | ¾ c. ea.: sugar, vinegar,
   | cooking wine
   | ⅓ c. ea.: soy sauce, lemon
   | juice
   | 1 T. ea.: salt, Szechuan
   | pepper-corns (or ½ t.
   | pepper)
   | 3 red chili peppers
   | 3 ea.: green onions, ginger
   | root slices

🐟　　🐟　　🐟

*15 pescados pequeños, 2⅔ lbs.
　(1200g)
6 C. maicena
aceite para freír*

① | *3 C. vino para cocinar*
   | *1¼ c. sal*

② | *1½ tz. agua*
   | *¾ tz. c/u: azúcar, vinagre, vino
   | para cocinar*
   | *⅓ tz. c/u: salsa de soya, jugo de
   | limón*
   | *1 C. c/u: sal, grano de pimienta
   | Szechuan (ó ½ c. pimienta)*
   | *3 chiles rojos*
   | *3 c/u: cebollines, rebanadas de
   | raíz de jengibre*

1️⃣ 魚於肉厚處劃刀痕，加 ① 料醃10分鐘拭乾，沾太白粉備炸。② 料燒開備用。

2️⃣ 「炸油」燒熱，放入魚炸約6分鐘呈金黃色撈出，趁熱泡入 ② 料內，待涼置冰箱續泡24小時以上（泡時需翻面），可隨時取食（可保存4-5天）。

☐ 炸魚時宜分數次炸，以免魚粘在一起。

🐟　　🐟　　🐟

1️⃣ Score fish in thick areas; marinate in ① for 10 minutes; pat dry; coat with cornstarch; set aside. Bring ② to boil; set aside.

2️⃣ Heat oil for deep-frying. Deep-fry fish until golden, about 6 minutes; remove. Soak the fried fish while hot in ②; let cool; refrigerate and keep soaking for at least 24 hours (turn over during soaking). Serve anytime (can be refrigerated for 4 to 5 days).

☐ Deep-fry the fish a few at a time to prevent sticking together.

🐟　　🐟　　🐟

1️⃣ *Haga cortes al pescado en las áreas gruesas; marine en ① por 10 minutos; seque ligeramente; cubra con maicena; deje aparte. Haga hervir ②; deje aparte.*

2️⃣ *Caliente bastante aceite para freír. Fría el pescado hasta que esté dorado, como 6 minutos; retire. Remoje el pescado frito mientras esté caliente en ②; deje enfriar; refrigere y déjelo remojar por lo menos 24 horas (voltee mientras se remoja). Sirva cuando quiera (se puede refrigerar por 4 ó 5 días).*

☐ *Fría pocos pescados a la vez para que no se peguen.*

酥小魚　　　　　　Crispy Small Fish
Pescado Pequeño Crujiente

小魚約15條 .. 1200公克（2斤）
「炸油」 .... 適量

醬油 1大匙
酒 3大匙
鹽 1小匙

蔥末、薑末 各1½大匙
蒜末、辣椒末(或辣椒醬)各1大匙

酒、醬油、醋 各2大匙
糖、麻油 各1大匙
水 2大匙

🐟　　🐟　　🐟

**15 small fish, 2⅔ lbs. (1200g)
oil for deep-frying**

**1 T. soy sauce
3 T. cooking wine
1 t. salt**

**1½ T. ea.(minced): green
onions, ginger root
1 T. ea.(minced):garlic
cloves, chili pepper (or
chili sauce)**

**2 T. ea.: cooking wine, soy
sauce, vinegar
1 T. ea.: sugar, sesame oil
2 T. water**

🐟　　🐟　　🐟

*15 pescados pequeños, 2⅔ lbs.
(1200g)
aceite para freír*

*1 C. salsa de soya
3 C. vino para cocinar
1 c. sal*

*1½ C. c/u (finamente picado):
cebollín, raíz de jengibre
1 C. c/u (finamente picado):
dientes de ajo, chile (o salsa
de chile)*

*2 C. c/u: vino para cocinar,
salsa de soya, vinagre
1 C. c/u: azúcar, aceite de
sésamo
2 C. agua*

1 魚於肉厚處劃刀痕，加 **1** 料醃10分鐘後拭乾備炸。

2 「炸油」燒熱，放入魚以中小火炸約6分鐘至魚酥脆後撈出。

3 油1大匙燒熱，炒香 **2** 料隨入 **3** 料及魚炒拌至汁收乾即可。冷吃熱食均可。

☐ 肉鯽、小鯽魚、小黃魚、小銀魚等均適合做醋浸魚或酥小魚。

🐟　　🐟　　🐟

1 Score fish in thick areas; marinate in **1** for 10 minutes; pat dry before deep-frying.

2 Heat oil for deep-frying. Deep-fry fish over medium-low heat until crispy and crunchy, about 6 minutes; remove.

3 Heat 1 T. oil; stir-fry **2** until fragrant; stir in **3** and fried fish until liquid has evaporated; remove. Serve hot or cold.

☐ Japanese butterfish, small silver carp, small yellow croaker, small silver fish are all suitable for this recipe or for the recipe of "Fish with Vinegar Sauce."

🐟　　🐟　　🐟

1 *Haga cortes en las áreas gruesas del pescado; marine en* **1** *por 10 minutos; seque ligeramente antes de freír.*

2 *Caliente bastante aceite para freír. Fría el pescado a fuego moderado-bajo hasta que esté crujiente y quebradizo, como 6 minutos; retire.*

3 *Caliente 1 C. de aceite; fría-revolviendo* **2** *hasta que esté aromático; agregue revolviendo* **3** *y el pescado frito hasta que el líquido se haya evaporado; retire. Sirva caliente o frío.*

☐ *Pampanito japonés, carpa plateada pequeña, roncador amarillo pequeño, pez plateado pequeño son todos adecuados para esta receta o para la receta "Pescado con Salsa de Vinagre."*

糖醋全魚

Sweet & Sour Fish

Pescado Agridulce

魚 .... 600公克（1斤）
蛋黃 1個
太白粉 1杯
「炸油」 .... 適量

① 鹽 .... ½小匙
　 酒 1大匙

② 洋蔥絲 .... ¼杯
　 青、紅甜椒絲 .... 共¼杯

③ 糖、醋、水 各6大匙
　 番茄醬 6大匙
　 鹽 .... ¼小匙
　 太白粉 .... ½小匙

🐟　🐟　🐟

1 whole fish, 1⅓ lbs. (600g)
1 egg yolk
1 c. cornstarch
oil for deep-frying

① ½ t. salt
　 1 T. cooking wine

② ¼ c. shredded onion
　 ¼ c. total (shredded): green
　 and red bell peppers

③ 6 T. ea.: sugar, vinegar,
　 water
　 6 T. ketchup
　 ¼ t. salt
　 ½ t. cornstarch

🐟　🐟　🐟

1 pescado entero, 1⅓ lbs.
　 (600g)
1 yema de huevo
1 tz. maicena
aceite para freír

① ½ c. sal
　 1 C. vino para cocinar

② ¼ tz. cebolla picada
　 ¼ tz. en total (cortado en
　 tajas): pimientos verdes y
　 rojos

③ 6 C. c/u: azúcar, vinagre, agua
　 6 C. catsup
　 ¼ c. sal
　 ½ c. maicena

1

① 　魚身兩面每隔1.5公分切斜刀深觸及骨，加 ① 料醃20分鐘拭乾，炸前依序塗上蛋黃，沾裹太白粉，魚身各處需仔細敷緊。

② 　「炸油」燒至九分熱，提起魚尾入鍋，並用鍋鏟淋熱油於魚身，使魚身花紋定型，續以中火炸約10分鐘至外皮酥脆，取出置盤。

③ 　油2大匙炒香 ② 料，隨入拌勻 ③ 料煮滾，淋於魚上。亦可使用帶魚（圖1）。

🐟　🐟　🐟

① 　Make diagonal cuts through the meat to the bone every ⅝" (1.5cm) on both sides of the fish; marinate in ① for 20 minutes; pat dry. Before frying, coat fish and inside cuts with egg yolk, then with cornstarch thoroughly.

② 　Heat oil to high for deep-frying. Hold the fish by its tail; gently lower into wok; slide through the oil; deep-fry. Spatula hot oil over the fish during frying to firm up the cuts; continue deep-frying over medium heat until skin on both sides is crispy, about 10 minutes; remove; transfer to a serving plate.

③ 　Heat 2 T. oil; stir-fry ② until fragrant; add mixture ③ ; cook until boiling; sprinkle over the fish; serve. This recipe is excellent when using ribbonfish (Fig. 1).

🐟　🐟　🐟

① 　*Haga cortes diagonales de la carne al hueso cada ⅝" (1.5cm) por ambos lados del pescado; marine en ① por 20 minutos; seque ligeramente. Antes de freír, cubra el pescado y los cortes internos con la yema de huevo, luego cúbralo completamente con maicena.*

② 　*Caliente bastante aceite para freír. Sujete el pescado de la cola, bájelo con cuidado a la sartén wok; pase por el aceite; fríalo. Con una espátula vacíele aceite caliente al pescado mientras se fríe para endurecer los cortes; continúe friendo a fuego moderado hasta que la piel de ambos lados esté crujiente, como 10 minutos; retire; ponga en el plato a servir.*

③ 　*Caliente 2 C. de aceite; fría-revolviendo ② hasta que esté aromático; agregue la mezcla ③ ; cocine hasta que hierva; vacíe sobre el pescado; sirva. Esta receta es excelente si usa anguileta del mar (Fig. 1).*

松鼠魚 **Squirrel-Patterned Fish**

Pescado con Patrón de Ardilla

魚 .... 600公克（1斤）
蛋黃 1個
太白粉 1杯
「炸油」 .... 適量

① 、③ 料同左

② 洋蔥丁、紅蘿蔔丁、青豆仁共½杯

❧　　❧　　❧

1⅓ lbs. (600g) fish
1 egg yolk
1 c. cornstarch
oil for deep-frying

① and ③ are the same as ingredients ① and ③ of left page "Sweet & Sour Fish"

② ½ c. total: diced onions, diced carrots, green peas

❧　　❧　　❧

1⅓ lbs. (600g) pescado
1 yema de huevo
1 tz. maicena
aceite para freír

① *y* ③ *son como los ingredientes de* ① *y* ③ *de la página izquierda "Pescado Agridulce"*

② *½ tz. en total: cebolla picada, zanahoria picada, chícharos*

① 將魚由背部下刀，順大骨切開，去除中間大骨（見第8頁魚肉切割法），並使魚腹相連攤開成一大片。

② 在魚肉面劃菱形刀紋後，加 ① 料醃20分鐘拭乾，依序塗上蛋黃，沾裹太白粉，再參照糖醋全魚做法將魚炸呈金黃色外皮酥脆撈起。

③ 油2大匙燒熱，炒香 ② 料，隨入拌勻的 ③ 料煮成濃稠狀，淋在魚上即可。

❧　　❧　　❧

① Butterfly the fish by sliding the blade along backbone; remove the backbone (see p. 8 for cutting). Do not cut through belly; open fish out in one flat piece.

② Make crisscross cuts on both sides of the fish; marinate in ① for 20 minutes; pat dry. Coat fish with egg yolk, then with cornstarch. Follow procedure ② of "Sweet & Sour Fish" (p. 36) to deep-fry fish until skin on both sides is golden and crispy; remove.

③ Heat 2 T. oil; stir-fry ② until fragrant; add mixture ③ ; stir until liquid has thickened; sprinkle over the fish; serve.

❧　　❧　　❧

① *Corte el pescado en forma de mariposa pasando el cuchillo por la espina dorsal; quítele la espina dorsal (vea p. 8 para cortar). No corte por el estómago; abra el pescado en una pieza plana.*

② *Haga cortes en forma de equis por ambos lados del pescado; siga el mismo procedimiento* ② *de "Pescado Agridulce" p. 36: fría el pescado hasta que la piel de ambos lados esté dorada y crujiente; retire.*

③ *Caliente 2 C. de aceite; fría-revolviendo* ② *hasta que esté aromático; agregue la mezcla* ③ *; revuelva hasta que el líquido espese; vacíe sobre el pescado; sirva.*

腐皮海鮮捲　Bean Curd Rolls with Seafood
Rollos de Tofu con Mariscos

豆腐皮 3張
「炸油」 .... 適量

① 魚漿 .... 225公克（6兩）
　絞肉 .... 115公克（3兩）
　酒、糖 各1大匙
　鹽、胡椒 .... 各¼小匙

② 中蝦仁 12條
　香腸或洋火腿 1½條
　紅蘿蔔絲 4大匙
　韭菜或菠菜（燙熟） 6棵

③ 蛋 1個
　麵粉 2大匙

3 bean curd skins
oil for deep-frying

① ½ lb.(225g) fish cake
¼ lb.(115g) ground meat
1 T. ea.: cooking wine,
　sugar
¼ t. ea.: salt, pepper

② 12 medium size shelled
　shrimp
1½ sausage or ham
4 T. shredded carrots
6 bunches cooked
　Chinese chives or
　spinach

③ 1 egg, 2 T. flour

3 hojas de tofu
aceite para freír

① ½ lb. (225g) pasta de pescado
¼ lb. (115g) carne molida
1 C. c/u: vino para cocinar,
　azúcar
¼ c. c/u: sal, pimienta

② 12 camarones medianos
　pelados
1½ salchicha o jamón
4 C. zanahoria rallada
6 manojos cocidos de
　cebollines chinos o espinaca

③ 1 huevo, 2 C. harina

1

1 ① 料拌勻分成3份。蝦仁加少許鹽略醃，香腸1條直剖成四小條。將豆腐皮先抹上一份拌勻之 ① 料，中間擺一份 ② 料（圖1）捲起成長條狀。

2 「炸油」燒熱，將腐皮捲沾上拌勻的 ③ 料，入鍋用小火先炸5分鐘，再改大火炸2分鐘呈金黃色，肉熟皮酥即可撈起切塊置盤，沾胡椒鹽或番茄醬食用。

□ ② 料內的材料可隨自己喜好改用墨魚、筍或香菇等。

1 Mix ① until blended; divide into 3 portions. Marinate the shrimp with a pinch of salt; let stand briefly. Cut one sausage lengthwise into 4 strips. Place one portion of ① on a bean curd skin. Place one portion of ② on the center of ① (Fig. 1). Roll up the skin sheet to form a baton. Follow the same procedure to make the other rolls.

2 Heat oil for deep-frying. Coat the bean curd rolls with mixture ③; deep-fry over low heat for 5 minutes first; increase heat to high; deep-fry the bean curd rolls for another 2 minutes until done, golden, and crispy; remove and cut into pieces; place on a plate and serve with pepper-salt or ketchup.

□ Cuttlefish, bamboo shoots, or Chinese black mushrooms may be substituted for ingredients in ② .

1 *Revuelva ① hasta que se mezcle; divida en 3 porciones. Marine los camarones con una pizca de sal; deje brevemente. Corte una salchicha a lo largo en 4 tiras. Coloque una porción de ① en una hoja de tofu. Coloque una porción de ② en el centro de ① (Fig. 1). Enrolle la hoja formando una batuta. Siga el mismo procedimiento para preparar los otros rollos.*

2 *Caliente bastante aceite para freír. Reboce los rollos con la mezcla ③; fríalos sobre fuego bajo primero por 5 minutos; aumente el fuego a alto; fría los rollos por otros 2 minutos hasta que estén listos, dorados, y crujientes; retire y corte en pedazos; coloque en un plato y sirva con sal pimienta o catsup.*

□ *Se puede substituir jibia, brotes de bambú u hongos chinos negros por los ingredientes en ② .*

雞捲
Rollos de Tofu

Bean Curd Rolls

豆腐皮（15公分×20公分）..6張
「炸油」.......................... 適量

1. 魚漿 .... 6兩（225公克）
   絞肉 .... 6兩（225公克）

2. 洋蔥（切碎）................ 1½ 杯
   紅蘿蔔（切碎）.............. ½ 杯

3. 糖 ...... 1½ 大匙，鹽 ...... ⅓小匙
   酒 1大匙
   麻油 1小匙
   胡椒 .... 少許
   太白粉 2大匙

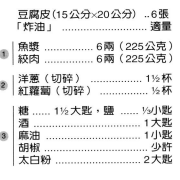

6 bean curd skins
  (6"×8",15cm×20cm)
oil for deep-frying

1. ½ lb.(225g) fish paste
   ½ lb.(225g) ground meat

2. 1½ c. chopped onions
   ½ c. chopped carrots

3. 1½ T. sugar, ⅓ t. salt
   1 T. cooking wine
   1 t. sesame oil
   dash of pepper
   2 T. cornstarch

6 hojas de tofu (6" × 8", 15cm
*   × 20cm)*
aceite para freír

1. *½ lb. (225g) pasta de pescado*
   ½ lb. (225g) carne molida

2. *1½ tz. cebolla picada*
   ½ tz. zanahoria picada

3. *1½ C. azúcar, ⅓ c. sal*
   1 C. vino para cocinar
   1 c. aceite de sésamo
   pizca de pimienta
   2 C. maicena

1 將 ❶ 、❷ 及 ❸ 料拌勻成餡，每張腐皮上置 ⅙ 份餡，捲成長條狀備炸。

2 炸油燒熱，將腐皮捲用小火先炸4分鐘後，改大火炸2分鐘至皮酥肉熟即可撈起切小段，沾番茄醬或胡椒鹽食用。

炸魚餅 將拌勻的雞捲餡用手擠成丸子，沾裹麵包粉後做成圓餅狀，入燒熱油鍋中以中火炸3-4分鐘至熟撈起，沾料食用。

1 To prepare filling: Mix ❶, ❷, and ❸ until blended. Divide the filling into 6 portions. Put one portion of filling in the center of each bean curd skin. Roll the skins to form cylinders.

2 Heat the oil for deep-frying. Deep-fry bean curd rolls over low heat, 4 minutes; increase heat to high; deep-fry for another 2 minutes until done and crispy; remove; cut into small sections; serve with pepper-salt or ketchup.

Deep-Fried Fish Patties Squeeze mixtures ❶, ❷, and ❸ with hands to form balls; coat with bread crumbs; press with hands to form patties. Heat oil for deep-frying; deep-fry over medium heat 3 to 4 minutes until done; remove. Serve with a dip.

1 *Para preparar el relleno: Combine ❶, ❷ y ❸ hasta que esté mezclado. Divida el relleno en 6 porciones. Coloque una porción del relleno en el centro de cada hoja de tofu. Enrolle las hojas en forma de cilindros.*

2 *Caliente bastante aceite para freír. Fría los rollos en bastante aceite sobre fuego lento, 4 minutos; aumente el fuego a alto; fría por otros 2 minutos hasta que estén listos y crujientes; retire; corte en secciones pequeñas; sirva con sal pimienta o catsup.*

Tortas Fritas de Pescado *Apriete las mezclas ❶, ❷ y ❸ con las manos para formar bolas; cubra con pan desmenuzado; aplane con las manos formando tortas. Caliente bastante aceite para freír; fría sobre fuego moderado de 3 a 4 minutos hasta que estén listas; retire. Sirva con un dip.*

炸魚餅 · Deep-Fried Fish Patties
Tortas Fritas de Pescado

韮黃炒魚條 Fish Strips & Yellow Chives

Tiras de Pescado y Cebollines Amarillos

4人份 · serves 4
4 porciones

魚肉 .... 225公克（6兩）
韮黃或豆芽 ..... 225公克（6兩）

① 鹽 .... ¼小匙
酒、太白粉 .... 各½大匙

② 醬油 2大匙
糖、麻油 .... 各½小匙
太白粉 1小匙
水 2大匙

③ 蔥花、蒜末 各2大匙

½ lb.(225g) fish fillet
½ lb.(225g) Chinese yellow
  chives or bean sprouts

① ¼ t. salt
½ T. ea.: cooking wine,
  cornstarch

② 2 T. soy sauce
½ t. ea.: sugar, sesame oil
1 t. cornstarch
2 T. water

③ 2 T.ea.: chopped green
  onion, minced garlic
  cloves

½ lb. (225g) filete de pescado
½ lb. (225g) cebollines chinos
  amarillos o brotes de soya

① ¼ c. sal
½ C. c/u: vino para cocinar,
  maicena

② 2 C. salsa de soya
½ c. c/u: azúcar, aceite de
  sésamo
1 c. maicena
2 C. agua

③ 2 C. c/u: cebollines picados,
  dientes de ajo finamente
  picados

---

① 魚肉切長條，調 **①** 料，炒前拌油1大匙，則炒時魚肉較易炒開。韮黃切段。

② 油½杯燒熱，將魚肉以過油方式小心拌炒至九分熟取出，留油2大匙入韮黃速炒二、三下，隨入拌勻的 **②** 料及魚條迅速炒拌，盛盤，中間留一凹洞，填入 **③** 料，並以燒熱的油澆在蔥、蒜上，可隨喜好加薑絲、香菜一起拌食。

---

① Cut fish fillet into strips; marinate in **①** . Mix with 1 T. oil before stir-frying to separate fish easily during cooking. Cut Chinese yellow chives in sections.

② Heat ½ c. oil; slide fish through oil; stir-fry gently until almost done; remove. Ladle off and reserve 2 T. oil in the wok; add chives; spatula chives 2 to 3 times quickly; add mixture **②** and fish; quickly stir-fry until combined; transfer to a plate. Make a well in center of the dish; pour **③** into well; sprinkle bubbling hot oil over green onions and garlic. Serve with shredded ginger and coriander, if desired.

---

① Corte los filete en tiras; marine en **①** . Mezcle con 1 C. de aceite antes de freír-revolviendo para que el pescado se separe fácilmente cuando se cocina. Corte los cebollines chinos amarillos en secciones.

② Caliente ½ tz, de aceite; deslice el pescado en el aceite; fría-revolviendo cuidadosamente hasta que esté casi listo; retire. Saque el aceite a cucharadas dejando 2 C. de aceite en la sartén wok; agregue los cebollines y revuelva 2 ó 3 veces rápidamente; agregue la mezcla **②** y el pescado; fría-revolviendo rápidamente hasta que esté combinado; coloque en un plato. Haga un pozo en el centro del plato; vacíe **③** en el pozo; rocíe aceite caliente burbujando sobre los cebollines y el ajo. Sirva con jengibre rallado y cilantro, si gusta.

西芹炒魚條　　Fish Strips & Celery

Tiras de Pescado y Apio

4人份 · serves 4
4 porciones

魚肉	....	225公克（6兩）
薑	....	3片

①
鹽	....	¼小匙
酒、太白粉	....	各¾大匙
蛋白	....	½個

②
西洋芹菜、熟紅蘿蔔	....
.... 共225公克（6兩）

③
醬油	....	1大匙
糖	....	½小匙
鹽、胡椒	....	各¼小匙
太白粉	....	1小匙
水	....	3大匙

🍃　🍃　🍃

½ lb.(225g) fish fillet
3 slices ginger root

①
¼ t. salt
¾ T. ea.: cooking wine, cornstarch
½ egg white

②
½ lb. (225g) total: celery, cooked carrots

③
1 T. soy sauce
½ t. sugar
¼ t. ea.: salt, pepper
1 t. cornstarch
3 T. water

🍃　🍃　🍃

½ lb. (225g) filete de pescado
3 rebanadas raíz de jengibre

①
¼ c. sal
¾ C. c/u: vino para cocinar, maicena
½ clara de huevo

②
½ lb. (225g) en total: apio, zanahorias cocidas

③
1 C. salsa de soya
½ c. azúcar
¼ c. c/u: sal, pimienta
1 c. maicena
3 C. agua

1️⃣ 魚肉切粗條，調 ① 料後拌油1大匙。西芹切段，紅蘿蔔切條備用。

2️⃣ 油½杯燒熱，入魚肉以過油方式小心拌炒至九分熟取出，留油2大匙，爆香薑片，再入 ② 料略炒並加水2大匙蓋鍋煮至水蒸氣冒出，隨入魚片及調勻 ③ 料炒拌均勻即可。

☐ 魚肉拌入蛋白、太白粉調味，可保滑嫩。

🍃　🍃　🍃

1️⃣ Cut fish fillet into thick strips; marinate in ① then in 1 T. oil. Cut celery in sections and carrots in strips; set aside.

2️⃣ Heat ½ c. oil; slide fish through oil; stir-fry gently until almost done; remove. Ladle off and reserve 2 T. oil in wok; stir-fry ginger slices until fragrant; add ② ; stir-fry briefly; add 2 T. water; cover and cook until steaming; stir in fish strips with mixture ③ until blended; serve.

☐ Coat fish fillet with egg white and cornstarch to keep fish at their tenderest and juiciest best.

🍃　🍃　🍃

1️⃣ *Corte los filete de pescado en tiras gruesas; marine en ① luego en 1 C. de aceite. Corte el apio en secciones y las zanahorias en tiras; deje aparte.*

2️⃣ *Caliente ½ tz. de aceite; deslice el pescado en el aceite; fría-revolviendo cuidadosamente hasta que esté casi listo; retire. Saque el aceite a cucharadas dejando 2 C. de aceite en la sartén wok; fría-revolviendo las rebanadas de jengibre hasta que esté aromático; agregue ② ; fría-revolviendo brevemente; agregue 2 C. de agua; tape y cocine hasta que se evapore; agregue revolviendo las tiras de pescado con la mezcla ③ hasta que se mezcle; sirva.*

☐ *Cubra los filetes de pescado con la clara de huevo y maicena para mantener el pescado tierno y jugoso.*

松子魚丁　　Diced Fish & Pine Nuts
Cubos de Pescado y Piñones

魚肉 .... 300公克（8兩）
松子（圖1）...................... ½杯

①
鹽 .... ¼小匙
酒、太白粉 各1大匙

②
蔥花 1大匙
薑末 1小匙

③
水 2大匙
鹽、糖 .... 各¼小匙
麻油 .... ½小匙
胡椒 .... ⅛小匙
太白粉 1小匙

🍃　🍃　🍃

⅔ lb. (300g) fish fillet
½ c. pine nuts (Fig.1)

①
¼ t. salt
1 T. ea.: cooking wine,
**　　cornstarch**

②
1 T. chopped green onions
1 t. minced ginger root

③
2 T. water
¼ t. ea.: salt, sugar
½ t. sesame oil
⅛ t. pepper
1 t. cornstarch

🍃　🍃　🍃

⅔ lb. (300g) filete de pescado
½ tz. piñones (Fig. 1)

①
¼ c. sal
1 C. c/u: vino para cocinar,
**　　maicena**

②
1 C. cebollín picado
1 c. raíz de jengibre finamente
**　　picada**

③
2 C. agua
¼ c. c/u: sal, azúcar
½ c. aceite de sésamo
⅛ c. pimienta
1 c. maicena

1 魚肉切小丁，調 **①** 料，炒前拌油1大匙，則炒時魚肉較易炒開。

2 松子放入½杯冷油內，小火慢炸約3分鐘，需時時攪動至呈淺黃色時撈出。

3 油2大匙炒香 **②** 料，入魚丁炒熟，並以調勻 **③** 料炒勻撒上炸好松子即成。

☐ 松子亦可以腰果、核桃替代。

🍃　🍃　🍃

1 Dice fish fillet; mix in **①** ; mix in 1 T. oil before frying to separate fish easily during cooking.

2 Place pine nuts in ½ c. cold oil; deep-fry over low heat about 3 minutes, stirring constantly until lightly browned; remove.

3 Heat 2 T. oil; stir-fry **②** until fragrant; add diced fish; stir-fry until done; stir in mixture **③** until combined; sprinkle with fried pine nuts; serve.

☐ Cashew nuts and walnuts can be substituted for pine nuts.

🍃　🍃　🍃

1 *Corte los filete en cubos; mezcle en* **①** *; agregue 1 C. de aceite antes de freír para que el pescado se separe fácilmente cuando se fría.*

2 *Coloque los piñones en ½ tz. de aceite frío; fría en bastante aceite a fuego bajo como 3 minutos, revolviendo constantemente hasta que estén poco dorados; retire.*

3 *Caliente 2 C. de aceite; fría-revolviendo* **②** *hasta que esté aromático; agregue los cubos de pescado; fría-revolviendo hasta que esté listo; agregue revolviendo la mezcla* **③** *hasta que se combine; espolvoree con los piñones fritos; sirva.*

☐ *Puede substituir anacardos y nueces por los piñones.*

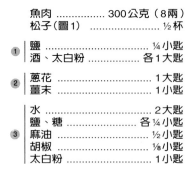

1

乾椒魚丁　　Diced Fish & Chili Pepper

Cubos de Pescado y Chile

4人份 · serves 4
4 porciones

魚肉 .... 300公克（8兩）
熟花生米 .... 適量

① 鹽 .... ¼ 小匙
酒、太白粉 各1大匙

② 乾辣椒（去籽切段）........... ¼ 杯
蔥段（3公分長） 6段
薑末 1小匙

③ 醬油 2大匙
糖、醋 各1大匙
麻油 .... ½ 大匙
太白粉 .... 1小匙，水 3大匙

❧　　❧　　❧

**⅔ lb. (300g) fish fillet
roasted peanuts as desired**

① ¼ t. salt
1 T. ea.: cooking wine,
cornstarch

② ¼ c. dried red chili pepper,
seeded and cut in sections
6 green onion sections,
1¼" (3cm) long
1 t. minced ginger root

③ 2 T. soy sauce
1 T. ea.: sugar, vinegar
½ T. sesame oil
1 t. cornstarch, 3 T. water

❧　　❧　　❧

**⅔ lb. (300g) filete de pescado
cacahuates tostados al gusto**

① ¼ c. sal
1 C. c/u: vino para cocinar,
maicena

② ¼ tz. chiles rojos secos, sin
semillas y cortados en
secciones
6 secciones de cebollines, 1¼ "
(3cm) de largo
1 c. raíz de jengibre finamente
picada

③ 2 C. salsa de soya
1 C. c/u: azúcar, vinagre
½ C. aceite de sésamo
1 c. maicena, 3 C. agua

1 魚肉切2公分大丁，調 **①** 料後，炒前拌油1大匙，則炒時魚肉較易炒開。

2 油½杯燒至八分熱，入魚丁翻炒至變色撈出，留油2大匙，炒香 **②** 料，隨入魚丁及調勻的 **③** 料炒勻盛盤，亦可與花生米配食。

☐ 乾辣椒（圖1）以中火炒過才香，應避免炒焦，否則會有苦味。

❧　　❧　　❧

1 Dice fish fillet into ¾" (2cm) pieces; marinate in **①** ; mix in 1 T. oil before stir-frying to separate fish easily during cooking.

2 Heat ½ c. oil to medium high; stir-fry fish until color changes; remove. Ladle off and reserve 2 T. oil in wok; stir-fry **②** until fragrant; return cooked fish to wok; stir in mixture **③** until combined; serve with peanuts if desired.

☐ The dried chili pepper (Fig. 1) will be aromatic after being stir-fried over medium heat. Avoid over-browning to prevent a bitter taste.

❧　　❧　　❧

1 *Corte los filete en cubos de ¾" (2cm); marine en **①** ; agregue 1 C. de aceite antes de freír-revolviendo para que el pescado se separe fácilmente cuando se cocine.*

2 *Caliente ½ tz. de aceite a fuego mediano-alto; fría-revolviendo el pescado hasta que cambie de color; retire. Saque el aceite a cucharadas dejando 2 C. de aceite en la sartén wok; fría-revolviendo **②** hasta que esté aromático; regrese el pescado cocido a la sartén; agregue revolviendo la mezcla **③** hasta que se combine; sirva con cacahuates si gusta.*

☐ *El chile seco (Fig. 1) estará aromático después de freír-revolviendo a fuego moderado. No lo fría demasiado para prevenir un sabor amargo.*

1

豆醬魚丁　Diced Fish in Bean Sauce

Cubos de Pescado en Salsa de Tofu

魚肉 .... 225公克（6兩）
嫩薑絲 2大匙

① 黃豆醬或味噌 3大匙
　 糖 .... ½小匙
　 水 1杯

② 蔥花 2大匙
　 味精 .... 隨意

❧　　❧　　❧

½ lb. (225g) fish fillet
2 T. shredded baby ginger
　　root

① 3 T. fermented soy bean
　　paste or miso
　 ½ t. sugar, 1 c. water

② 2 T. chopped green onions

❧　　❧　　❧

*½ lb. (225g) filete de pescado
2 C. raíz de jengibre pequeña
　　rallada*

① *3 C. pasta de tofu fermentada o
　　miso
　½ c. azúcar, 1 tz. agua*

② *2 C. cebollín picado*

1 魚肉切小丁，① 料調勻備用。

2 油2大匙燒熱，炒香薑絲，入魚肉炒開，隨入 ① 料煮滾，拌入 ② 料即可。

☐ 此道菜做法簡單，可拌飯食用。

❧　　❧　　❧

1 Dice fish fillet. Mix ① thoroughly; set aside.

2 Heat 2 T. oil; stir-fry shredded ginger until fragrant; stir in fish until separated; add ① and bring to boil; mix with ② ; serve.

☐ This easy-to-make dish goes well with rice.

❧　　❧　　❧

1 *Corte los filete de pescado en cubos. Mezcle ① completamente; deje aparte.*

2 *Caliente 2 C. de aceite; fría-revolviendo el jengibre rallado hasta que esté aromático; agregue revolviendo el pescado hasta que se separe; agregue ① y haga hervir; mezcle con ② ; sirva.*

☐ *Este plato tan fácil de preparar se complementa bien con arroz.*

醬汁魚片　Sliced Fish in Chili Sauce

Rebanadas de Pescado en Salsa Picante

魚肉 .... 225公克（6兩）
薑末 1小匙

1. 鹽 .... ¼小匙
酒、太白粉 各1大匙

2. 熟紅蘿蔔片、洋菇片、豌豆莢 ....
.... 共1杯

3. 辣醬油 2大匙
糖、麻油 .... 各½小匙

❧　❧　❧

½ lb.(225g) fish fillet
1 t. minced ginger root

1. ¼ t. salt
1 T. ea.: cooking wine, cornstarch

2. 1 c. total: cooked and sliced carrots, sliced mushrooms, Chinese pea pods

3. 2 T. chili soy sauce
½ t. ea.: sugar, sesame oil

❧　❧　❧

½ lb. (225g) filete de pescado
1 c. raíz de jengibre finamente picada

1. *¼ c. sal*
1 C. c/u: vino para cocinar, maicena

2. *1 tz. en total: zanahoria cocida en rebanadas, hongos rebanados, hojas de chícharos chinos*

3. *2 C. salsa de soya con chile*
½ c. c/u: azúcar, aceite de sésamo

1. 魚肉切成3公分×4公分×1公分厚片，加 ① 料醃10分鐘。

2. 油2大匙燒熱，鍋離火將魚片排入，再置回爐上將魚煎至兩面呈金黃色魚肉熟取出，餘油炒香薑末，入 ② 料略炒，再入魚片及 ③ 料炒拌即刻起鍋。

❧　❧　❧

1. Cut the fillet into 1¼" × 1½" × ½" (3cm × 4cm × 1cm) thick slices; marinate in ① for 10 minutes.

2. Heat 2 T. oil; remove the frying pan from heat; spread fish slices in the pan; return pan to heat; pan-fry fish until done and golden on both sides; remove. Stir-fry minced ginger with remaining oil until fragrant; add ② and stir-fry briefly; return pan-fried fish; stir in mixture ③ until blended; remove immediately.

❧　❧　❧

1. *Corte el filete en pedazos gruesos de 1¼" × 1½" × ½" (3cm × 4cm × 1cm); marine en ① por 10 minutos.*

2. *Caliente 2 C. de aceite; quite la sartén del fuego; acomode los pedazos de pescado en la sartén; regrese la sartén al fuego; fría el pescado hasta que esté listo y dorado por ambos lados; retire. Fría-revolviendo el jengibre en el aceite restante hasta que esté aromático; agregue ② y fría-revolviendo brevemente; regrese el pescado frito; agregue revolviendo la mezcla ③ hasta que se combine; retire inmediatamente.*

烤烏魚子
Barbecued Mullet Roe

烏魚子 1付
酒 3大匙
蒜苗（切薄片） 2支
或蒜（切片） 10粒

🍃　　🍃　　🍃

**1 pair of mullet roe
3 T. cooking wine**

**2 fresh garlic spears
(sliced) or 10 slices
garlic cloves**

1 烏魚子用濕布擦淨，兩面塗酒備用。如烏魚子太乾需加酒浸泡5分鐘（泡時需翻面）。

2 火烤法：以小火慢烤至外層微焦，表面鼓起一粒粒小泡，香味四溢時即可。
烘烤法：乾鍋燒熱，將烏魚子以小火邊烘烤邊翻面，邊刷酒至兩面微黃並有香味，中間微熟即可。

3 烤好烏魚子切薄片，可依喜好裝盤，與 1 料或白蘿蔔片同食，沾檸檬汁或醋也別有風味。

🐋　　🐋　　🐋

1 Clean mullet roe with damp cloth; brush wine on both sides; set aside. If roe is too dry, soak in wine for 5 minutes (turn over during soaking process).

2 Barbecuing: Barbecue mullet roe over low heat until the surface is lightly browned, bubbly, and aromatic.
Stove top barbecuing: Heat a pan; heat roe in pan over low heat constantly turning over and brushing on wine to lightly brown on both sides, fragrant, and slightly warm in center.

3 Slice mullet roe thinly; arrange on a plate according to your taste; serve with 1 and white radish slices. For extra flavor, serve with lemon juice or vinegar.

Hueva de Mújol a la Barbacoa

Fotos a la izq.

4 porciones

1 par de hueva de mújol
3 C. vino para cocinar

① 2 brotes enteros de ajo
(rebanados) ó 10 dientes de
ajo

1 *Limpie la hueva de mújol con un trapo húmedo; con una brocha cepille vino por ambos lados; deje aparte. Si la hueva está muy reseca, sumerja en vino por 5 minutos (voltee mientras la remoja).*

2 *Barbacoa: Cueza la hueva de mújol estilo barbacoa a fuego bajo hasta que la superficie esté ligeramente dorada, burbujante, y aromática. Barbacoa sobre la estufa: Caliente la sartén; caliente la hueva a fuego bajo volteando y cepillando con vino constantemente mientras se calienta hasta que esté ligeramente dorada por ambos lados, aromática, y un poco caliente en el centro; retire.*

3 *Corte la hueva de mújol en rebanadas delgadas; acomode en un plato a su gusto; sirva con ① y rebanadas de rábano blanco. Para darle más sabor, sirva con jugo de limón o vinagre.*

煎烏魚鰾

Fried Mullet Bladder

Vejiga de Mújol Frita

4人份 · serves 4

4 porciones

烏魚鰾 .... 225公克（6兩）

① 蔥（3公分長）................. 6段
紅辣椒（切片）................. 1條

② 醬油 3大匙
酒 2大匙
糖 .... ½大匙
味精 .... 隨意

1 烏魚鰾選大而色白者較佳，洗淨瀝乾。

2 油3大匙燒熱，以大火將魚鰾兩面煎呈金黃色，鏟於鍋邊，餘油炒香 ① 料，隨入 ② 料及魚鰾燒煮2分鐘後，淋上麻油½大匙即可。

½ lb. (225g) mullet bladder

① 6 green onion sections,
1¼" (3cm) long
1 red chili pepper, sliced

② 3 T. soy sauce
2 T. cooking wine
½ T. sugar

½ lb. (225g) vejiga de mújol

① 6 secciones de cebollín, 1¼"
(3cm) de largo
1 chile rojo, rebanado

② 3 C. salsa de soya
2 C. vino para cocinar
½ C. azúcar

1 Opt for large, white mullet bladder; clean and pat dry.

2 Heat 3 T. oil; pan-fry bladder over high heat until golden on both sides; spatula to the side of wok; add ① and stir-fry until fragrant; add ② and spatula mullet bladder back to the center; mix well; cook 2 minutes; sprinkle with ½ T. sesame oil; serve.

1 *Opte por vejiga de mújol blanca y grande; limpie y seque ligeramente.*

2 *Caliente 3 C. de aceite; fría la vejiga en la sartén a fuego alto hasta que se dore por ambos lados; con una espátula muévala a un lado de la sartén wok; agregue ① y fría-revolviendo hasta que esté aromático; agregue ② y con la espátula regrese la vejiga de mújol al centro; mezcle bien; cocine por 2 minutos; rocíe con ½ C. de aceite de sésamo; sirva.*

五味鱈魚　　　　　　　　**Five-Spice Codfish**

Bacalao con Cinco Especias

鱈魚 .... 300公克（8兩）
太白粉 2大匙

①
鹽 .... ¼小匙
酒 1小匙

②
蔥、蒜末 各2大匙
薑末、紅辣椒片 .... 各½大匙
醬油、黑醋 各1½大匙
糖 .... ½小匙
冷開水 1大匙

❧　　❧　　❧

⅔ lb.(300g) codfish
2 T. cornstarch

①
¼ t. salt
1 t. cooking wine

②
2 T. ea.(minced):green
onions, garlic cloves
½ T.ea.:minced ginger
root, sliced red chili
pepper
1½ T. ea.: soy sauce, black
vinegar
½ t. sugar
1 T. cold water

❧　　❧　　❧

⅔ lb. (300g) bacalao
2 C. maicena

①
¼ c. sal
1 c. vino para cocinar

②
2 C. c/u, (finamente picado):
cebollín, dientes de ajo
½ C. c/u: raíz de jengibre
finamente picada, chile rojo
rebanado
1½ C. c/u: salsa de soya,
vinagre negro
½ c. azúcar
1 C. agua fría

1 鱈魚切1.5公分厚大片，加 **①** 料醃10分鐘後，沾上太白粉備用。

2 油2大匙燒熱，入魚片煎至兩面呈金黃色並熟，迅速淋上調勻的 **②** 料即成。

☐ 將煎熟之魚片置燒熱的鐵板上，迅速淋上調味醬即為鐵板鱈魚。（鐵板具有保溫之功效）。

❧　　❧　　❧

1 Cut codfish into ⅝" (1.5cm) thick slices; marinate in **①** for 10 minutes; coat with cornstarch; set aside.

2 Heat 2 T. oil; pan-fry fish until done and golden on both sides; sprinkle with mixture **②** quickly; serve.

☐ Codfish Cooked in Cast-Iron Plate: Place pan-fried fish on heated cast-iron plate; sprinkle sauce over quickly; serve (cast-iron plate is used to keep dish warm).

❧　　❧　　❧

1 *Corte el bacalao en pedazos de ⅝" (1.5cm) de grueso; marine en* **①** *por 10 minutos; reboce con maicena; deje aparte.*

2 *Caliente 2 C. de aceite; fría el pescado en la sartén hasta que esté listo y dorado por ambos lados; vacíele la mezcla* **②** *rápidamente; sirva.*

☐ *Bacalao Cocido en un Plato de Hierro: Coloque el pescado que se frió en la sartén sobre un plato de hierro caliente; vacíele la salsa encima rápidamente; sirva (se usa un plato de hierro para mantener caliente el platillo).*

麻辣魚塊　Grass Carp & Chili Pepper

Carpa con Chile

草魚 .... 300公克（8兩）
太白粉 1大匙

① 鹽 .... ¼小匙
酒 1大匙

② 蒜末 1大匙
醬油、紅辣椒（切片）各2大匙
糖、麻油 .... 各½小匙

🐚　　🐚　　🐚

⅔ lb.(300g) grass carp
1 T. cornstarch

① ¼ t. salt
1 T. cooking wine

② 1 T. minced garlic cloves
2 T. ea.: soy sauce, red
chili pepper (sliced)
½ t. ea.: sugar, sesame oil

🐚　　🐚　　🐚

⅔ lb. (300g) carpa
1 C. maicena

① ¼ c. sal
1 C. vino para cocinar

② 1 C. dientes de ajo finamente
picados
2 C. c/u: salsa de soya, chile
rojo rebanado
½ c. c/u: azúcar, aceite de
sésamo

1　魚切2公分厚片，加 ① 料醃10分鐘後，沾太白粉備用。

2　油3大匙燒至九分熱，魚入鍋（不可馬上翻面）以中火煎並轉動鍋子以防燒焦，約2分鐘至魚皮微黃肉稍熟，再翻面同法煎約5分鐘至肉熟且呈金黃色，取出盛盤。餘油入 ② 料煮滾，淋於魚上即成。

🐚　　🐚　　🐚

1　Cut fish into ¾" (2cm) thick pieces; marinate in ① for 10 minutes; coat with cornstarch.

2　Heat 3 T. oil to high; place fish in wok (do not turn fish over right away); lower heat to medium; tilt pan and pan-fry to prevent burning until skin is lightly browned and flesh is almost cooked through, about 2 minutes; turn over; pan-fry 5 minutes until done and golden; remove; transfer to a plate. Cook ② with remaining oil until boiling; pour over fish; serve.

🐚　　🐚　　🐚

1　*Corte el pescado en pedazos de ¾" (2cm) de grueso; marine en ① por 10 minutos; reboce con maicena.*

2　*Caliente 3 C. de aceite a fuego alto; coloque el pescado en la sartén wok (no voltee el pescado inmediatamente); baje el fuego a moderado; ladee la sartén y fríalo sin que se queme hasta que la piel esté un poco dorada y la carne esté casi cocida por dentro, como 2 minutos; voltee; fría por 5 minutos hasta que esté listo y dorado; retire; ponga en un plato. Cocine ② con el aceite restante hasta que hierva; vacíe sobre el pescado; sirva.*

洋蔥魚排 Fried Fish with Onions
Pescado Frito con Cebolla

魚肉 .... 300公克（8兩）
洋蔥 .... 225公克（6兩）

① 鹽 .... ¼小匙
酒、太白粉 各1大匙

② 紅辣椒末 1大匙
番茄醬 3大匙
黑醋、醬油 各1大匙
檸檬汁、糖 .... 各½大匙
水 3大匙

⋙　⋙　⋙

²⁄₃ lb.(300g) fish fillet
½ lb.(225g) onions

① ¼ t. salt
1 T. ea.: cooking wine,
cornstarch

② 1 T. minced red chili pepper
3 T. ketchup
1 T. ea.: black vinegar, soy
sauce
½ T. ea.: lemon juice,
sugar
3 T. water

⋙　⋙　⋙

²⁄₃ lb. (300g) filete de pescado
½ lb. (225g) cebollas

① ¼ c. sal
1 C. c/u: vino para cocinar,
maicena

② 1 C. chile rojo finamente
picado
3 C. catsup
1 C. c/u: vinagre negro, salsa
de soya
½ C. c/u: jugo de limón,
azúcar
3 C. agua

① 魚肉切1公分厚片，加 ① 料醃10分鐘，洋蔥切絲備用。

② 油3大匙燒熱，入魚片以中大火煎至兩面呈金黃色並熟取出。

③ 油2大匙燒熱，入洋蔥炒香，先取出一半置盤上，再入調勻的 ② 料燒開，隨入魚片略拌盛於洋蔥上即可。

⋙　⋙　⋙

① Cut fillet into ½" (1cm) thick pieces; marinate in ① for 10 minutes. Shred onions; set aside.

② Heat 3 T. oil; pan-fry fish slices over medium-high heat until done and golden; remove.

③ Heat 2 T. oil; stir-fry onions until fragrant; remove half of the onions and transfer to a serving plate; add mixture ② to wok; bring to boil; mix in fish briefly; pour over the onion-bedded plate; serve.

⋙　⋙　⋙

① *Corte el filete en pedazos de ½" (1cm) de grueso; marine en ① por 10 minutos. Corte las cebollas; deje aparte.*

② *Caliente 3 C. de aceite; fría los pedazos de pescado en la sartén a fuego moderado alto hasta que estén listos y dorados; retire.*

③ *Caliente 2 C. de aceite; fría-revolviendo la cebolla hasta que esté aromática; saque la mitad de la cebolla y ponga en el plato a servir; agregue la mezcla ② a la sartén wok; haga hervir; agregue el pescado mezclando brevemente; vacíe sobre la cebolla que está en el plato; sirva.*

Filetes de Pescado con Pimienta

4人份・serves 4
4 porciones

鱈魚 .... 300公克（8兩）
洋蔥末 .... ¼ 杯

1
鹽 .... ¼ 小匙
酒 .... 1 大匙

2
黑胡椒、蒜末 .... 各½ 大匙
高湯 .... ½ 杯
醬油 .... 1½ 大匙
麻油 .... 1 小匙
味精 .... 隨意
太白粉 .... 1 小匙

⅔ lb.(300g) codfish
¼ c. minced onions

1
¼ t. salt
1 T. cooking wine

2
½ T. ea.: black pepper,
  minced garlic cloves
½ c. stock
1 ½ T. soy sauce
1 t. sesame oil
1 t. cornstarch

⅔ lb. (300g) bacalao
¼ tz. cebolla finamente picada

1
¼ c. sal
1 C. vino para cocinar

2
½ C. c/u: pimienta negra,
  dientes de ajo finamente
  picados
½ tz. caldo
1½ C. salsa de soya
1 c. aceite de sésamo
1 c. maicena

1 魚肉切1.5公分厚片，加 **1** 料醃10分鐘瀝乾。油3大匙燒熱，入魚片以中火煎至金黃色並熟取出置盤上備用。

2 油2大匙燒熱，炒香洋蔥，隨入調勻的 **2** 料煮滾，淋於魚上即可。

□ 魚排亦可蒸或烤熟後淋上煮滾 **2** 料。**2** 料亦可以現成黑胡椒醬取代。

1 Cut fish into ⅝" (1.5cm) thick pieces; marinate in **1** for 10 minutes; drain. Heat 3 T. oil; pan-fry fish over medium heat until done and golden; remove; transfer to a serving plate; set aside.

2 Heat 2 T. oil; stir-fry onions until fragrant; add mixture **2** ; bring to boil; pour over the fish.

□ You may steam or bake fish steaks then pour cooked mixture **2** over the fish. Ready-made black pepper sauce may be substituted for ingredients **2** .

1 *Corte el pescado en pedazos de ⅝" (1.5cm) de grueso; marine en* **1** *por 10 minutos; escurra. Caliente 3 C. de aceite; fría en la sartén a fuego moderado hasta que esté listo y dorado; retire; ponga en el plato a servir; deje aparte.*

2 *Caliente 2 C. de aceite; fría-revolviendo la cebolla hasta que esté aromática; agregue la mezcla* **2** *; haga hervir; vacíe sobre el pescado.*

□ *Puede hornear los filetes o cuézalos al vapor luego vacíe la mezcla* **2** *cocida sobre el pescado. Salsa de pimienta negra ya preparada se puede substituir por los ingredientes de* **2** *.*

Pescado en Vinagre Estilo Taiwanés　4人份・serves 4
4 porciones

魚 .... 600公克（1斤）

① 酒 1大匙
　 鹽 .... ½小匙

② 醬油 3大匙
　 黑醋或白醋 2大匙
　 麻油、糖 .... 各½大匙
　 薑末、蒜末 .... 各½大匙
　 蔥末 2大匙
　 辣椒（切片） 1條

🍵　　🍵　　🍵

1⅓ lbs. (600g) fish

① **1 T. cooking wine**
　 ½ t. salt

② **3 T. soy sauce**
　 2 T. black or white vinegar
　 ½ T. ea.: sesame oil, sugar
　 **½ T.ea.(minced): ginger
　　 root, garlic cloves**
　 2 T. minced green onions
　 1 red chili pepper, sliced

🍵　　🍵　　🍵

1⅓ lbs. (600g) pescado

① *1 C. vino para cocinar*
　 ½ c. sal

② *3 C. salsa de soya*
　 2 C. vinagre negro o blanco
　 *½ C. c/u: aceite de sésamo,
　　 azúcar*
　 *½ C. c/u, (finamente picado):
　　 raíz de jengibre, dientes de
　　 ajo*
　 2 C. cebollín finamente picado
　 1 chile rojo rebanado

1　魚在肉厚處劃刀痕，加 ① 料醃20分鐘，煎前拭乾。

2　油3大匙燒熱，放入魚以中火煎約7分鐘至兩面呈金黃色，魚肉熟皮酥脆時鏟起盛盤。將調好的 ② 料趁熱淋上即成。

香醋烹魚　魚片調 ① 料並加太白粉1大匙略醃，將魚煎呈金黃色，隨入 ② 料即刻盛盤。

🍵　　🍵　　🍵

1　Score fish in thick areas; marinate in ① for 20 minutes; pat dry before pan-frying.

2　Heat 3 T. oil; pan-fry fish over medium high heat until done and golden and the skin is crispy on both sides, 7 minutes; transfer to a serving plate. While fish is still hot, pour on mixture ② ; serve.

Fried Vinegar Fish Marinate fish pieces in ① and 1 T. cornstarch briefly; pan-fry fish until golden; sprinkle on mixture ② ; transfer to a plate immediately; serve.

🍵　　🍵　　🍵

1　*Haga cortes en las áreas gruesas del pescado; marine en ① por 20 minutos; seque ligeramente antes de freír.*

2　*Caliente 3 C. de aceite; fría el pescado en la sartén a fuego moderado alto hasta que esté listo y dorado y la piel esté crujiente por ambos lados, 7 minutos; ponga en el plato a servir. Vacíe la mezcla ② al pescado caliente; sirva.*

Pescado Frito en Vinagre *Marine los pedazos de pescado en ① y reboce en 1 C. de maicena brevemente; fría en la sartén hasta que esté dorado; vacíele la mezcla ② ; ponga en un plato inmediatamente; sirva.*

香醋烹魚・Fried Vinegar Fish
Pescado Frito en Vinagre

五柳魚 — Five-Vegetable Fish
Pescado con Cinco Vegetales

4人份 · serves 4
4 porciones

魚 .... 600公克（1斤）
太白粉 1大匙
肉絲 .... ⅓杯

① | 酒 .... 1大匙，鹽 .... ⅔小匙

② | 蝦米（泡軟） 1大匙
香菇絲......3朵，辣椒絲 1條

③ | 洋蔥絲 1杯
黃瓜絲、紅蘿蔔絲 .... 各⅓杯

④ | 高湯或水 .... 1¼ 杯
黑醋 .... 1¼ 大匙
糖.........¾ 大匙，鹽 1小匙
胡椒、麻油 .... 各少許
太白粉 1大匙

1⅓ lbs. (600g) fish
1 T. cornstarch
⅓ c. shredded meat

① | 1 T. cooking wine, ⅔ t. salt

② | 1 T. dried shrimp (soften in
water)
3 shredded Chinese black
mushrooms
1 shredded chili pepper

③ | 1 c. shredded onions
⅓ c. ea.(shredded):
cucumbers, carrots

④ | 1¼ c. stock or water
1¼ T. black vinegar
¾ T. sugar, 1 t. salt
dash of ea.: pepper, sesame
oil
1 T. cornstarch

1⅓ lbs. (600g) pescado
1 C. maicena
⅓ tz. carne deshebrada

① | 1 C. vino para cocinar, ⅔ c. sal

② | 1 C. camarón seco (remojado
en agua)
3 hongos negros chinos
rallados
1 chile picado

③ | 1 tz. cebolla rallada
⅓ tz. c/u, (rallado): pepino,
zanahoria

④ | 1¼ tz. caldo o agua
1¼ C. vinagre negro
¾ C. azúcar, 1 c. sal
pizca de pimienta, gotas de
aceite de sésamo
1 C. maicena

---

1 魚在肉厚處劃刀痕，加 ① 料醃20分鐘，拭乾沾裹太白粉。油3大匙燒熱，放入魚以中火煎約7分鐘，至兩面呈金黃色魚肉熟，鏟出置盤。
2 油3大匙燒熱，將 ② 料依序放入炒香，並將肉炒開至變色，隨入 ③ 料略炒後加 ④ 料攪拌燒開成濃稠狀，淋在魚上即成。
七星燒魚 油3大匙炒香蔥、薑，隨意加入香菇、筍、紅蘿蔔丁及青豆仁共1½杯略炒，並加 ④ 料燒開，淋在煎好魚上即可。

---

1 Score fish in thick areas; marinate in ① for 20 minutes. Remove and pat dry; coat with cornstarch. Heat 3 T. oil; pan-fry fish over medium heat until done and golden on both sides, about 7 minutes; transfer to a serving plate.
2 Heat 3 T. oil; add each ingredient in ② as listed into wok; stir-fry until fragrant; add meat and stir until separated and color changes; add ③ and stir-fry briefly; add ④; bring to boil and stir until mixture has thickened; sprinkle over the pan-fried fish.
Seven-Vegetable Fish Heat 3 T. oil; stir-fry green onions, ginger; liberally add 1½ c. of diced Chinese black mushrooms, diced bamboo, diced carrots, and green peas; stir briefly; add ④; bring to boil; sprinkle over pan-fried fish; serve.

---

1 Haga cortes en las áreas gruesas del pescado; marine en ① por 20 minutos. Saque y seque ligeramente; reboce con maicena. Caliente 3 C. de aceite; fría el pescado en una sartén a fuego moderado alto hasta que esté listo y dorado por ambos lados, como 7 minutos; ponga en el plato a servir.
2 Caliente 3 C. de aceite; agregue cada ingrediente de ② en ese orden en la sartén wok; fría-revolviendo hasta que esté aromático; agregue la carne y revuelva hasta que se separe y cambie de color; agregue ③ y fría-revolviendo brevemente; agregue ④; haga hervir y revuelva hasta que la mezcla espese; vacíe sobre el pescado frito.
Pescado con Siete Vegetales Caliente 3 C. de aceite; fría-revolviendo cebollines, jengibre; liberalmente agregue 1½ tz. hongos negros chinos picados, bambú picado, zanahoria picada, y chícharos, revuelva brevemente; agregue ④; haga hervir; vacíe sobre el pescado frito; sirva.

白杓魚片　Boiled Fish & Bean Threads
Pescado Hervido y Brotes de Soya

草魚或石斑魚肉300公克（8兩）
粉絲 1把

① 鹽 .... ¼小匙
　 酒、太白粉 各1大匙

② 水 6杯
　 酒 1大匙
　 蔥 .... 2支，薑 3片

③ 蔥絲、薑絲 各2大匙
　 紅辣椒絲 1大匙

④ 水 1杯
　 醬油 1½大匙
　 糖、胡椒 .... 各¼小匙
　 黑醋、麻油 各1小匙
　 太白粉 2小匙

🐟　🐟　🐟

⅔ lb.(300g) grass carp or
　 grouper fillet
1 bunch bean threads

① ¼ t. salt
　 1 T. ea.: cooking wine,
　 cornstarch

② 6 c. water, 2 green onions
　 1 T. cooking wine
　 3 ginger root slices

③ 2 T. ea.(shredded): green
　 onion, ginger root
　 1 T. shredded red chili
　 pepper

④ 1 c. water, 1½ T. soy sauce
　 ¼ t. ea.: sugar, pepper
　 1 t. ea.: black vinegar,
　 sesame oil
　 2 t. cornstarch

🐟　🐟　🐟

⅔ lb. (300g) filete de carpa o
　 mero
1 manojo de brotes de soya

① ¼ c. sal
　 1 C. c/u: vino para cocinar,
　 maicena

② 6 tz. agua, 2 cebollines
　 1 C. vino para cocinar
　 3 rebanadas raíz de jengibre

③ 2 C. c/u, (rebanado): cebollín,
　 raíz de jengibre
　 1 C. chile rojo picado

④ 1 tz. agua, 1½ C. salsa de soya
　 ¼ c. c/u: azúcar, pimienta
　 1 c. c/u: vinagre negro, aceite
　 de sésamo
　 2 c. maicena

① 魚肉切0.5公分厚片狀，加 ① 料醃10分鐘，粉絲燙熟墊盤底。

② 將 ② 料燒開，入魚片煮滾，見魚肉變色即刻撈出置粉絲上。油1大匙炒香 ③ 料，隨入拌勻的 ④ 料炒拌煮滾成濃汁，淋於魚上。

☐ 這道菜清爽簡單，魚肉宜選較不腥的魚，鱈魚肉易碎，較不適宜。

🐟　🐟　🐟

① Cut fillet into ¼" (0.5cm) thick slices; marinate in ① for 10 minutes; blanch bean threads in boiling water; line the plate with bean threads.

② Bring ② to boil; add fish slices; cook until color changes; remove immediately; place on top of bean threads. Heat 1 T. oil; stir-fry ③ until fragrant; add mixture ④; cook until combined and thickened; sprinkle over the fish; serve.

☐ This dish is crisp and easy to make. Opt for fish with a less offensive smell for this dish. Codfish is not suitable because it easily breaks apart.

🐟　🐟　🐟

① Corte el filete en rebanadas de ¼" (0.5cm) de grueso; marine en ① por 10 minutos; sumerja los brotes de soya en agua hirviendo; cubra el plato con los brotes de soya.

② Haga hervir ②; agregue las rebanadas de pescado; cocine hasta que cambie de color; retire inmediatamente; coloque sobre los brotes. Caliente 1 C. de aceite; fría-revolviendo ③ hasta que esté aromático; agregue la mezcla ④; cocine hasta que todo se combine y espese; vacíe sobre el pescado; sirva.

☐ Este platillo es crujiente y fácil de preparar. Opte por un pescado menos oloroso. No se recomienda bacalao porque se desbarata fácilmente.

咖哩魚片 Shark Fillets in Curry Sauce

Filetes de Tiburón en Salsa Curry

鯊魚肉 .... 300公克（8兩）
洋蔥片 1杯
咖哩粉 2小匙

① 鹽 .... ¼小匙
酒、太白粉 各1大匙

② 鹽 .... ⅓小匙
糖 .... ½小匙
太白粉 2小匙
水 1杯

⅔ lb.(300g) shark fillet
1 c. sliced onions
2 t. curry powder

① ¼ t. salt
1 T. ea.: cooking wine,
    cornstarch

② ⅓ t. salt
½ t. sugar
2 t. cornstarch
1 c. water

⅔ lb. (300g) filete de tiburón
1 tz. cebolla rebanada
2 c. polvo curry

① ¼ c. sal
1 C. c/u: vino para cocinar,
    maicena

② ⅓ c. sal
½ c. azúcar
2 c. maicena
1 tz. agua

① 魚肉切3公分×4公分×1公分薄片，以 ① 料醃10分鐘。

② 油4大匙燒熱，入魚片煎至兩面呈金黃色魚肉熟取出。餘油炒香洋蔥，再下咖哩粉略炒，隨入調勻的 ② 料炒拌均勻煮開後，再入魚肉略拌即可。

① Cut fillet into 1¼" × 1½" × ½" (3cm × 4cm × 1cm) thin slices; marinate in ① for 10 minutes.

② Heat 4 T. oil for pan-frying; pan-fry fillets until done and golden on both sides; stir-fry onions with remaining oil; stir in curry powder briefly; add mixture ② ; bring to boil; cook until mixture has thickened; return fish; stir briefly until combined; serve.

① Corte el filete en rebanadas de 1¼" × 1½" × ½" (3cm × 4cm × 1cm); marine en ① por 10 minutos.

② Caliente 4 C. de aceite para freír en la sartén; fría los filetes hasta que estén listos y dorados por ambos lados; fría-revolviendo la cebolla con el aceite restante; agregue el polvo curry mezclando brevemente; agregue la mezcla ② ; haga hervir; cocine hasta que la mezcla se espese; regrese el pescado; revuelva brevemente hasta que se combine; sirva.

糟溜魚片   Fish & Brewed Rice

Pescado y Vino de Arroz Fermentado

草魚或石斑魚肉300公克（8兩）
「炸油」 .... ½杯
酒釀（或酒） 1½大匙

①
酒 .... ½大匙
鹽 .... ⅓小匙
蛋白 .... ½個
太白粉 1大匙

② 蔥、薑末 各1大匙

③
鹽 .... ½小匙
高湯 .... ½杯
太白粉、糖 各1小匙

²⁄₃ lb.(300g) grass fish or
   grouper fillet
½ c. oil for deep-frying
1½ T. sweet brewed rice or
   cooking wine

①
½ T. cooking wine
⅓ t. salt
½ egg white
1 T. cornstarch

② 1 T. ea.(minced): green
   onions, ginger root

③
½ t. salt
½ c. stock
1 t. ea.: cornstarch, sugar

²⁄₃ lb. (300g) filete de mero
½ tz. aceite para freír
1½ C. vino de arroz dulce
   fermentado o vino para
   cocinar

①
½ C. vino para cocinar
⅓ c. sal
½ clara de huevo
1 C. maicena

② 1 C. c/u, (finamente picado):
   cebollín, raíz de jengibre

③
½ c. sal
½ tz. caldo
1 c. c/u: maicena, azúcar

1 魚肉斜切大薄片，加 **①** 料略醃。炒前再加油1大匙拌勻，則炒時魚片較易鏟開。

2 「炸油」燒熱，將魚肉放入泡熟撈出。留油2大匙炒香 **②** 料，隨加拌勻的 **③** 料，燒開後放入魚片及酒釀炒拌均勻即可。

1 Cut fillet diagonally into large thin pieces; marinate in **①** briefly. Mix in 1 T. oil before stir-frying to separate fish slices easily during cooking.

2 Heat oil for deep-frying. Deep-fry fish until cooked through; remove. Ladle off and reserve 2 T. oil in wok; stir-fry **②** until fragrant; add mixture **③**; bring to boil; stir in cooked fish and brewed rice; mix until blended; serve.

1 *Corte el filete diagonalmente en pedazos largos y delgados; marine en* **①** *brevemente. Agréguele 1 C. de aceite antes de freír-revolviendo para que el pescado se separe fácilmente al cocinar.*

2 *Caliente bastante aceite para freír. Fría el pescado hasta que se cocine completamente; retire. Saque el aceite a cucharadas dejando 2 C. de aceite en la sartén wok; fría-revolviendo* **②** *hasta que esté aromático; agregue la mezcla* **③**; *haga hervir; agregue el pescado cocido y el vino de arroz fermentado; revuelva hasta que se combine bien; sirva.*

檸檬魚片
Fish in Lemon Sauce
Pescado en Salsa de Limón

魚肉 .... 300公克（8兩）
「炸油」 .... 適量

① 酒 1大匙
鹽 .... ⅓小匙

② 蛋 1個
麵粉、太白粉、水 .... 各¼杯

③ 檸檬汁（或醋4大匙）、糖、水.......
.... 各5大匙
太白粉 .... ½大匙
鹽、麻油 .... 各½小匙

❧   ❧   ❧

⅔ lb.(300g) fish fillet
oil for deep-frying

① 1 T. cooking wine
⅓ t. salt

② 1 egg
¼ c. ea.: flour, cornstarch,
water

③ 5 T. ea.: lemon juice (or 4 T.
vinegar), sugar, water
½ T. cornstarch
½ t. ea.: salt, sesame oil

❧   ❧   ❧

⅔ lb. (300g) filete de pescado
aceite para freír

① 1 C. vino para cocinar
⅓ c. sal

② 1 huevo
¼ tz. c/u: harina, maicena,
agua

③ 5 C. c/u: jugo de limón (ó 4 C.
vinagre), azúcar, agua
½ C. maicena
½ c. c/u: sal, aceite de sésamo

1 魚肉切大薄片，加 ① 料拌勻。② 料拌勻成麵糊備用。

2 「炸油」燒熱，魚片沾裹麵糊入鍋炸呈金黃色，外皮酥脆後撈出，倒出油。③ 料入鍋，邊燒邊攪拌成濃稠狀，淋在魚片上即成。

醋溜魚片 將不同顏色蔬菜1杯略炒，加 ③ 料燒開，倒入炸好的魚片拌勻。

❧   ❧   ❧

1 Cut fillet into large, thin slices; marinate in ① thoroughly. Mix ② thoroughly to form flour batter; set aside.

2 Heat oil for deep-frying; dip the fish in the batter then deep-fry until golden and skin is crispy; remove. Remove oil; bring ③ to boil, stirring constantly until thickened; sprinkle over the fish and serve.

Fish in Vinegar Stir-fry 1 c. of assorted, colored vegetables briefly; add ③ ; bring to boil; spread over fried fish fillets; mix well; serve.

❧   ❧   ❧

1 *Corte el filete en rebanadas largas y delgadas; marine en ① completamente. Mezcle ② bien para formar el batido; deje aparte.*

2 *Caliente bastante aceite para freír; sumerja el pescado en el batido luego fría hasta que se dore y esté crujiente; retire. Saque el aceite; haga hervir ③ , revolviendo constantemente hasta que espese; rocíe sobre el pescado y sirva.*

Pescado en Vinagre *Fría-revolviendo brevemente 1 tz. de varios vegetales de varios colores; agregue ③ ; haga hervir; vacíe sobre los filetes de pescado frito; mezcle bien; sirva.*

醋溜魚片 · Fish in Vinegar
Pescado en Vinagre

酒燜鮮鮭魚　Simmered Salmon in Wine
Salmón en Vino

鮭魚 .... 300公克（8兩）
洋蔥、草菇或鮮香菇 ....
.... 共150公克（4兩）

1. 檸檬汁 1大匙
   鹽 ...... ¼小匙，胡椒 ..... ⅛小匙
2. 酒或紹興酒 .... ½杯
   醬油 1大匙
3. 芹菜末 1大匙
   酒 .... ½大匙

% % %

⅔ lb.(300g) fresh salmon
⅓ lb. (150g) total: onions,
   straw mushrooms or
   fresh Chinese black
   mushrooms

1. 1 T. lemon juice
   ¼ t. salt, ⅛ t. pepper
2. ½ c. cooking wine or Shao
   Hsing rice wine
   1 T. soy sauce
3. 1 T. chopped Chinese
   celery
   ½ T. cooking wine

% % %

⅔ lb. (300g) salmón fresco
⅓ lb. (150g) en total de
   cebollas, hongos con tallos u
   hongos negros chinos
   frescos

1. 1 C. jugo de limón
   ¼ c. sal, ⅛ c. pimienta
2. ½ tz. vino para cocinar o vino
   de arroz Shao Hsing
   1 C. salsa de soya
3. 1 C. apio chino picado
   ½ C. vino para cocinar

1　鮭魚切2公分厚片，加 ① 料醃10分鐘，洋蔥、草菇切片備用。

2　油2大匙燒熱，入洋蔥炒香，再入魚片、草菇及 ② 料以小火蓋鍋燜至魚肉熟約5分鐘，撒上 ③ 料即成。

檸汁燻鮭魚　燻鮭魚300公克（可在超市購買）切薄片排盤，上撒檸檬汁2大匙及胡椒少許即可，與洋蔥絲配食，是一道清爽的宴客菜。

% % %

1 Cut salmon into ¾" (2cm) thick slices; marinate in ① for 10 minutes. Slice onions and mushrooms for later use.

2 Heat 2 T. oil; stir-fry onions until fragrant; add fish slices, mushrooms, and ②; simmer over low heat until fish is cooked through, about 5 minutes; sprinkle on ③; serve.

Smoked Salmon in Lemon Juice Slice ⅔ lb. (300g) smoked salmon into thin slices; arrange on plate; top with 2 T. lemon juice; season with black pepper; serve with shredded onions. This is a crisp, formal dinner dish.

% % %

1 *Corte el salmón en pedazos de ¾" (2cm) de grueso; marine en ① por 10 minutos. Rebane las cebollas y los hongos para usar después.*

2 *Caliente 2 C. de aceite; fría-revolviendo la cebolla hasta que esté aromática; agregue los pedazos de pescado, hongos, y ②; cocine a fuego bajo hasta que el pescado esté cocido, como 5 minutos; espolvoree con ③; sirva.*

Salmón Ahumado en Jugo de Limón *Rebane ⅔ lb. (300g) de salmón ahumado en rebanadas; acomode en un plato; rocíe con 2 C. de jugo de limón; sazone con pimienta negra; sirva con cebolla rallada. Este es un platillo especial para una cena formal.*

檸汁燻鮭魚 · Smoked Salmon in Lemon Juice
Salmón Ahumado en Jugo de Limón

Pescado en Rollos de Alga

4人份 · serves 4
4 porciones

乾海帶（10公分長段）... 12段
鮪魚肉 .... 225公克（6兩）
干瓢（15公分長）.......... 12條

① 水 2杯
糖 2大匙
醋、醬油 各3大匙
薑 3片
酒 1大匙

ง   ง   ง

12 sections of dry
   seaweed, 4" (10cm) long
½ lb.(225g) tuna fillet
12 dried gourd strips
   (Kampyo) 6" (15cm) long

2 c. water
2 T. sugar
① 3 T. ea.: vinegar, soy sauce
3 ginger root slices
1 T. cooking wine

ง   ง   ง

12 secciones de alga marina
   seca, 4" (10cm) de largo
½ lb. (225g) filete de atún
12 tajadas de calabaza seca
   (Kampyo), 6" (15cm) de
   largo

2 tz. agua
2 C. azúcar
① *3 C. c/u: vinagre, salsa de soya*
3 rebanadas raíz de jengibre
1 C. vino para cocinar

① 海帶沖水洗淨，魚肉切2公分×2公分×5公分之長條12條，干瓢（圖1）泡軟備用。

② 取海帶一段，上鋪魚條捲起，並以干瓢綁緊，入燒開的 ① 料待滾後，蓋鍋以小火煮約30分鐘，至汁將收乾即可。

☐ 煮時略搖動鍋子以防燒焦。此菜味濃可熱食或冷食，適合當小菜或便當菜。

ง   ง   ง

1 Clean seaweed under cold running water; cut fillet into twelve ¾" × ¾" × 2" (2cm × 2cm × 5cm) long sections. Soak dried gourd strips (Fig. 1) in water until softened.

2 Place a fish section on top of a seaweed section; fold to make a roll and tie with a gourd strip; make eleven more rolls in the same manner; bring ① to boil; drop fish rolls in water; cover and cook over low heat until liquid has almost evaporated, about 30 minutes; serve.

☐ To prevent burning; shake the pot gently during cooking. This dish has a rich flavor and can be served hot or cold. Also it may be served as an hors d'oeuvre or packed for lunch.

ง   ง   ง

1 *Lave el alga marina bajo el agua fría de la llave; corte el filete en 12 secciones de ¾" × ¾" × 2" (2cm × 2cm × 5cm) de largo. Remoje las tajadas de la calabaza seca (Fig. 1) en agua hasta que se ablanden.*

2 *Coloque una sección de pescado sobre cada sección de alga; doble formando un rollo y amarre con una tira de calabaza; haga los otros 11 rollos de la misma manera; haga hervir ① ; suelte los rollos de pescado en agua; tape y cubra a fuego bajo hasta que el líquido se haya casi evaporado, como 30 minutos; sirva.*

☐ *Para que no se quemen; agite la olla cuidadosamente durante la cocción. Este platillo tiene un rico sabor y se puede servir caliente o frío. También se puede servir como aperitivo o llevar para el almuerzo.*

1

乾燒魚

Spicy Fried Fish

Pescado Frito Picante

魚 ....600公克（1斤）
「炸油」 ....適量

1. 酒 1大匙
   鹽 .... ½ 小匙

2. 蔥花 .... ½ 杯
   薑、蒜末 各1大匙

3. 番茄醬 3大匙
   豆瓣醬 1小匙

4. 水 .... ¾ 杯，鹽 .... ¾ 小匙
   糖、酒、麻油 各1大匙
   太白粉 .... ½ 大匙

ⅈ	ⅈ	ⅈ

1⅓ lbs.(600g) fish
oil for deep-frying

1. 1 T. cooking wine
   ½ t. salt

2. ½ c. chopped green onions
   1 T. ea.(minced): ginger
   root, garlic cloves

3. 3 T. ketchup
   1 t. chili sauce

4. ¾ c. water, ¾ t. salt
   1 T. ea.: sugar, cooking
   wine, sesame oil
   ½ T. cornstarch

ⅈ	ⅈ	ⅈ

1⅓ lb. (600g) pescado
aceite para freír

1. 1 C. vino para cocinar
   ½ c. sal

2. ½ tz. cebolla picada
   1 C. c/u, (finamente picado):
   raíz de jengibre, dientes de
   ajo

3. 3 C. catsup
   1 c. salsa de chile

4. ¾ tz. agua, ¾ c. sal
   1 C. c/u: azúcar, vino para
   cocinar, aceite de sésamo
   ½ C. maicena

1. 魚在肉厚處劃刀痕，加 ❶ 料略醃。❷、❸、❹ 料分別備妥。

2. 「炸油」燒熱，放入魚炸至金黃色肉熟鏟出置盤。

3. 油4大匙燒熱，炒香 ❷、❸ 料，隨入 ❹ 料炒拌成濃稠狀淋在魚上（圖1）即可。

ⅈ	ⅈ	ⅈ

1. Score fish in thick areas; marinate in ❶ briefly. Mix ❷, ❸, and ❹ in separate bowls.

2. Heat oil for deep-frying; fry fish until done and golden on both sides; remove and put on a serving plate.

3. Heat 4 T. oil; stir-fry ❷ and ❸ until fragrant; stir in ❹ until combined and thickened; sprinkle over the fish (Fig. 1); serve.

ⅈ	ⅈ	ⅈ

1. *Haga cortes en las áreas gruesas del pescado; marine en ❶ brevemente. Mezcle ❷, ❸, y ❹ en tazones separados.*

2. *Caliente bastante aceite para freír; fría el pescado hasta que esté listo y dorado por ambos lados; retire y ponga en el plato a servir.*

3. *Caliente 4 C. de aceite; fría-revolviendo ❷ y ❸ hasta que esté aromático; agregue revolviendo ❹ hasta que se combine y espese; vacíe sobre el pescado (Fig. 1); sirva.*

1

Pescado y Tomates

沙丁魚 .... 450公克（12兩）
洋蔥 .... 75公克（2兩）
番茄 .... 150公克（4兩）

酒、醋 各1大匙
鹽 .... ½小匙
醬油 .... ½大匙
薑末 1小匙
番茄汁 1杯

ꕤ　　ꕤ　　ꕤ

1 lb. (450g) sardines
2½ oz. (75g) onion
⅓ lb. (150g) tomatoes

1 T. ea.: cooking wine,
　　vinegar
½ t. salt
½ T. soy sauce
1 t. minced ginger root
1 c. tomato juice

ꕤ　　ꕤ　　ꕤ

1 lb. (450g) sardinas
2½ oz. (75g) cebolla
⅓ lb. (150g) tomates

1 C. c/u: vino para cocinar,
　　vinagre
½ c. sal
½ C. salsa de soya
1 c. raíz de jengibre finamente
　　picada
1 tz. jugo de tomate

1 魚處理乾淨，濾乾水份。洋蔥、番茄切碎備用。

2 油2大匙燒熱，炒香洋蔥，入番茄略炒，隨入魚及 **1** 料煮滾，改小火燜煮約15分鐘即成。

□ 沙丁魚可用鯖魚或炸彈魚取代。

ꕤ　　ꕤ　　ꕤ

1 Clean the fish; drain. Finely chop onions and tomatoes for later use.

2 Heat 2 T. oil; stir-fry onions until fragrant; add tomatoes and stir-fry briefly; add fish and **1**; bring to boil; reduce heat to low; simmer for 15 minutes; serve.

□ Mackerel and round frigate mackerel may be substituted for sardines.

ꕤ　　ꕤ　　ꕤ

1 *Lave el pescado, escurra. Pique la cebolla y tomate finamente para usar después.*

2 *Caliente 2 C. de aceite; fría-revolviendo la cebolla hasta que esté aromática; agregue los tomates y fría-revolviendo brevemente; agregue el pescado y* **1** *; haga hervir; baje el fuego a lento; cocine a fuego lento por 15 minutos; sirva.*

□ *Caballa y caballa fragata redonda puede substituirse por las sardinas.*

豆瓣鯰魚   Catfish & Bean Sauce

Bagre y Salsa de Frijol

4人份・serves 4
4 porciones

鯰魚 .... 600公克（1斤）

① 辣豆瓣醬 1大匙
   蔥、薑、蒜末 各1大匙

② 酒、醬油 各1½大匙
   醋、糖 .... 各½大匙
   鹽 .... ½小匙，水 1½杯
   味精 .... 少許

③ 太白粉 .... 1大匙，水 2大匙

④ 蔥花 3大匙
   麻油 1大匙

🦐   🦐   🦐

1⅓ lbs.(600g) catfish

① **1 T. chili bean paste**
1 T. ea.(minced):green onions, ginger root, garlic cloves

② **1½ T. ea.: cooking wine, soy sauce**
½ T. ea.: vinegar, sugar
½ t. salt, 1½ c. water

③ **1 T. cornstarch, 2 T. water**

④ **3 T. chopped green onions**
1 T. sesame oil

🦐   🦐   🦐

1⅓ lbs. (600g) bagre

① *1 C. pasta de frijol picante*
1 C. c/u, (finamente picado): cebollín, raíz de jengibre, dientes de ajo

② *1½ C. c/u: vino para cocinar, salsa de soya*
½ C. c/u: vinagre, azúcar
½ c. sal, 1½ tz. agua

③ *1 C. maicena, 2 C. agua*

④ *3 C. cebollín picado*
1 C. aceite de sésamo

1

1 鯰魚洗淨剁成兩段（圖1），拭乾。

2 油4大匙燒熱，將魚兩面煎黃約2分鐘取出或鏟至鍋邊，炒香 **①** 料，再將魚移至鍋中，加 **②** 料蓋鍋用中火燒煮6分鐘（煮時需翻面）至魚肉熟，汁剩約一半時將魚盛出置盤，餘汁以 **③** 料勾成濃汁並加 **④** 料，淋在魚上。

☐ 也可將麵煮熟放在魚旁，與醬汁拌食。

🦐   🦐   🦐

1 Clean the catfish, cut in half (Fig. 1); pat dry.

2 Heat 4 T. oil; pan-fry fish until golden, about 2 minutes; spatula to the side of wok; stir-fry **①** until fragrant; spatula the fish back to the center; add **②**; cover and cook 6 minutes over medium heat (turn over during cooking), until fish is cooked through and juice has reduced to half; transfer fish only to a serving plate. Thicken the juice remaining in wok with mixture **③**; add **④**; pour over the fish and serve.

☐ Cooked noodles can be served on the side; pour bean paste sauce over the dish.

🦐   🦐   🦐

1 *Limpie el bagre, corte por la mitad (Fig. 1); seque ligeramente.*

2 *Caliente 4 tz. de aceite; fría el pescado en la sartén hasta que esté dorado, como 2 minutos; muévalo a un lado de la sartén wok; fría revolviendo **①** hasta que esté aromático; regrese el pescado al centro; agregue **②**; tape y cueza por 6 minutos a fuego moderado (voltee durante la cocción), hasta que el pescado esté bien cocido y el jugo se haya reducido a la mitad; coloque solamente el pescado en el plato a servir. Espese el jugo restante de la sartén con la mezcla **③**; agregue **④**; vacíe sobre el pescado y sirva.*

☐ *Se puede servir tallarines cocidos al lado; vacíe la salsa de la pasta de frijol sobre el platillo.*

豆瓣魚燒豆腐　Spicy Fish & Bean Curd
Pescado Picante y Tofu

魚	300公克（8兩）
鹽	¼小匙
豆腐	300公克（1盒）
蔥花	2大匙

① 蔥、薑、蒜末 各1大匙
辣豆瓣醬（圖1）............ 1大匙

② 鹽 1小匙
醬油 1大匙
糖、醋 .... 各½大匙
水 1½杯

③ 太白粉 1大匙
水 1大匙

☙　☙　☙

⅔ lb.(300g) fish
¼ t. salt
⅔ lb. (300g) bean curd
2 T. chopped green onions

① 1 T. ea. (minced): green
　　onions, ginger root,
　　garlic cloves
1 T. chili bean paste (Fig.1)

② 1 t. salt, 1 T. soy sauce
½ T. ea.: sugar, vinegar
1½ c. water

③ 1 T. cornstarch
1 T. water

☙　☙　☙

⅔ lb. (300g) pescado
¼ c. sal
⅔ lb. (300g) tofu
2 C. cebollín picado

① 1 C. c/u, (finamente picado):
　　cebollín, raíz de jengibre,
　　dientes de ajo
1 C. pasta de frijol picante
　　(Fig. 1)

② 1 c. sal, 1 C. salsa de soya
½ C. c/u: azúcar, vinagre
1½ tz. agua

③ 1 C. maicena
1 C. agua

1

1 魚切塊加鹽略醃，豆腐切塊備用。

2 油3大匙燒熱，入魚塊以中火兩面煎黃盛出或鏟於鍋邊，餘油炒香 ❶ 料，再將魚置鍋中央，入豆腐及 ❷ 料，蓋鍋以中火燒煮約5分鐘，再以拌勻的 ❸ 料勾成濃汁，並撒蔥花盛於盤上即成。

☙　☙　☙

1 Cut fish in pieces then marinate in salt briefly. Cut bean curd in pieces; set aside.

2 Heat 3 T. oil; pan-fry fish over medium heat until done and golden on both sides; spatula to the side of wok; stir-fry ❶ with remaining oil until fragrant; spatula the fish back to the center; add bean curd and ❷; cover and cook over medium heat about 5 minutes; add mixture ❸ to thicken the juice; sprinkle with chopped green onions; transfer to a plate; serve.

☙　☙　☙

1 *Corte el pescado en pedazos luego marine en sal brevemente. Corte el tofu en pedazos; deje aparte.*

2 *Caliente 3 C. de aceite; fría el pescado a fuego moderado alto hasta que esté listo y dorado por ambos lados; muévelo al lado de la sartén wok; fría-revolviendo ❶ con el aceite restante hasta que esté aromático; regrese el pescado al centro de la sartén; agregue el tofu y ❷; tape y cocine a fuego moderado alto como 5 minutos; agregue la mezcla ❸ para espesar el jugo; espolvoree con el cebollín picado; vacíe en un plato; sirva.*

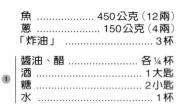

蔥燒魚　　　　　Fish & Green Onions

Pescado y Cebollines

4人份・serves 4
4 porciones

魚 .... 450公克（12兩）
蔥 .... 150公克（4兩）
「炸油」 3杯

① 醬油、醋 .... 各¼杯
　　酒 1大匙
　　糖 2小匙
　　水 1杯

ᴥ　　ᴥ　　ᴥ

1 lb. (450g) fish
⅓ lb. (150g) green onions
3 c. oil for deep-frying

① ¼ c. ea.: soy sauce,
　　vinegar
1 T. cooking wine
2 t. sugar
1 c. water

ᴥ　　ᴥ　　ᴥ

1 lb. (450g) pescado
⅓ lb. (150g) cebollines
3 tz. aceite para freír

① *¼ tz. c/u: salsa de soya,*
　　vinagre
1 C. vino para cocinar
2 c. azúcar
1 tz. agua

1️⃣ 魚去鰓、鱗及內臟洗淨，蔥切二段備用。

2️⃣ 「炸油」燒至九分熱，將魚炸約6分鐘至熟透並呈金黃色取出，留油3大匙入蔥段爆香至微黃，隨入魚及 ① 料一同煮開後，改小火蓋鍋燜煮約30分鐘至汁將收乾即可。

☐ 蔥燒魚傳統是以鯽魚來烹調，亦可以吳郭魚取代，材料較易取得，一樣可口。

ᴥ　　ᴥ　　ᴥ

1️⃣ Remove fish gills and entrails; rinse. Cut green onions in two sections.

2️⃣ Heat oil to high for deep-frying; deep-fry fish until golden, about 6 minutes; remove. Ladle off and reserve 3 T. oil in wok; stir-fry green onions until lightly browned and fragrant; return fish and add ① ; bring to boil; reduce heat to low; cover and simmer 30 minutes until juice has evaporated; serve.

☐ Traditionally, silver carp is used for this recipe. However, mouth breeder is easier to get in stores, just as tasty, and is a good substitute.

ᴥ　　ᴥ　　ᴥ

1️⃣ *Quítele las branquias y entrañas al pescado; enjuague. Corte los cebollines en secciones.*

2️⃣ *Caliente el aceite a fuego alto para freír; fría el pescado hasta que esté dorado, como 6 minutos; retire. Saque el aceite con una cuchara dejando 3 C. de aceite en la sartén wok; fría-revolviendo los cebollines hasta que estén ligeramente dorados y aromáticos; regrese el pescado y agregue ① ; haga hervir; baje el fuego a lento; tape y cocine a fuego lento por 30 minutos hasta que el jugo se haya evaporado; sirva.*

☐ *Tradicionalmente, se usa carpa plateada para esta receta. Sin embargo, merluza es más fácil de conseguir en la tienda, es igual de sabrosa, y es una buena substitución.*

燻魚

Pescado Ahumado

Smoked Fish

4人份 · serves 4
4 porciones

魚	1200公克（2斤）	
「炸油」	適量	
① 酒	3大匙	
鹽	1小匙	
② 蔥	2支	
薑	2片	
醬油	5大匙	
酒、糖	各4大匙	
紅辣椒	2條	
水	3杯	
醋	2小匙	

2⅔ lbs.(1200g) fish
oil for deep-frying

① **3 T. cooking wine**
1 t. salt

② **2 green onions**
2 slices ginger root
5 T. soy sauce
4 T. ea.: cooking wine,
sugar
2 red chili peppers
3 c. water
2 t. vinegar

2⅔ lbs. (1200g) pescado
aceite para freír

① *3 C. vino para cocinar*
1 c. sal

② *2 cebollines*
2 rebanadas raíz de jengibre
5 C. salsa de soya
4 C. c/u: vino para cocinar,
azúcar
2 chiles rojos
3 tz. agua
2 c. vinagre

1️⃣ 魚切2公分厚片，加 ① 料醃1小時，炸前拭乾。「炸油」燒熱，放入魚炸約6分鐘至酥脆後撈出。

2️⃣ 將 ② 料及炸好魚片同置鍋內，燒開後續煮15分鐘（煮時不需翻動以免魚肉破碎）至汁將收乾，淋上麻油2大匙，輕輕翻面再將汁收乾即可。

☐ 鯧魚、黃魚、石斑魚、鯉魚、草魚均適合做燻魚，可冷吃或做酒肴、便當菜。

1️⃣ Cut fish into ¾" (2cm) thick slices; marinate in ① for 1 hour; pat dry before deep-frying. Heat oil for deep-frying; deep-fry fish until crispy, about 6 minutes; remove.

2️⃣ Pour in ② and return fried fish to wok; bring to boil; continue cooking for 15 minutes (do not stir during cooking so fish will not break up) until juice has almost evaporated; sprinkle in 2 T. sesame oil; gently turn the fish over and cook until juice has evaporated; serve.

☐ Pomfret, yellow croaker, grouper, carp, and grass carp are all suitable for this recipe. It may be served as a cold dish or an hors d'oeuvre with wine. It can also be packed for lunch.

1️⃣ *Corte el pescado en pedazos de ¾" (2cm) de grueso; marine en ① por 1 hora; seque ligeramente antes de freír. Caliente bastante aceite para freír; fría el pescado hasta que esté crujiente, como 6 minutos; retire.*

2️⃣ *Agregue ② y regrese el pescado a la sartén wok; haga hervir; continúe cociendo por 15 minutos (no lo revuelva durante la cocción para no desbaratarlo) hasta que el jugo esté casi evaporado; rocíele 2 C. de aceite de sésamo; voltee el pescado con cuidado y cueza hasta que el líquido se evapore; sirva.*

☐ *Castañola, roncador amarillo, mero, y carpa son adecuados para esta receta. Se puede servir frío o como aperitivo con vino. También se puede llevar para el almuerzo.*

三杯魚

Pescado en Tres Salsas

虱目魚（切塊）　　300公克（8兩）
麻油 3大匙
薑 10片
九層塔 .... 適量
① ┌ 蒜 10粒
　 └ 紅辣椒（切片）........... 1條
② ┌ 酒 3大匙
　 └ 醬油 3大匙

☙　☙　☙

⅔ lb.(300g) milk fish, cut
　　into pieces
3 T. sesame oil
10 slices ginger root
fresh basil as desired

① ┌ 10 garlic cloves
　 └ 1 red chili pepper, sliced

② ┌ 3 T. cooking wine
　 └ 3 T. soy sauce

☙　☙　☙

⅔ lb. (300g) pez comestible,
　　cortado en pedazos
3 C. aceite de sésamo
10 rebanadas raíz de jengibre
albahaca fresca al gusto

① ┌ 10 dientes de ajo
　 └ 1 chile rojo, rebanado

② ┌ 3 C. vino para cocinar
　 └ 3 C. salsa de soya

Three-Sauce Fish

4人份 · serves 4
4 porciones

1 麻油燒熱，將薑片爆香，入魚塊以中火煎香，隨入 ① 料略炒，加 ② 料蓋鍋以中小火煮約4分鐘至汁將收乾，放入九層塔拌勻即可。

三杯鯰魚 虱目魚改用鯰魚，做法同上，但加 ② 料（② 料材料改為水1杯及醬油、酒各4大匙）後需燒煮約6分鐘，再加入泡軟粉絲續煮至汁將收乾即可。

☙　☙　☙

1 Heat sesame oil; stir-fry ginger slices until fragrant; pan-fry fish over medium heat until fragrant; stir in ① briefly; add ②; cover and cook over medium-low heat until juice has evaporated, about 4 minutes; mix with basil until combined; serve.

Three-Sauce Catfish Catfish may be substituted for milkfish. Follow the same procedure to make this dish. Increase cooking time to 6 minutes after adding ② (increase amount of ② to 1 c. water, 4 T. each of soy sauce and cooking wine); then add water-softened bean threads; continue cooking until juice has evaporated.

☙　☙　☙

1 *Caliente el aceite de sésamo; fría-revolviendo las rebanadas de jengibre hasta que esté aromático; fría el pescado en la sartén a fuego moderado alto hasta que esté aromático; agregue ① revolviendo brevemente; agregue ②; tape y cocine a fuego moderado hasta que el jugo se haya evaporado, como 4 minutos; mezcle con la albahaca hasta que se combine; sirva.*

Bagre en Tres Salsas *Puede substituir bagre por el pescado comestible. Siga el mismo procedimiento para preparar este platillo. Aumente el tiempo de la cocción a 6 minutos después de haber agregado ② (aumente la cantidad de ② con 1 tz. de agua, 4 C. c/u. de salsa de soya y vino para cocinar); luego agregue brotes de frijol ya ablandados en agua; continúe la cocción hasta que el jugo se haya evaporado.*

三杯鯰魚 · Three-Sauce Catfish
Bagre en Tres Salsas

九層塔燒魚
Pescado y Albahaca

Fish & Basil

4人份 · serves 4
4 porciones

虱目魚或吳郭魚450公克（12兩）
九層塔（圖1）................... ½ 杯

1 | 鹽 .... ½ 小匙
| 酒 .... 1 大匙

2 | 蔥段（3公分長）............... 6段
| 薑絲 .... 1 大匙

3 | 醬油 .... 2 大匙
| 糖 .... ½ 小匙
| 黑醋 .... 1 小匙
| 水 .... ¼ 杯

🐟   🐟   🐟

**1 lb.(450g) milk fish or
  mouth breeder
½ c. fresh basil (Fig.1)**

1 | ½ t. salt
| 1 T. cooking wine

2 | 6 green onion sections,
| 1¼" (3cm) long
| 1 T. shredded ginger root

3 | 2 T. soy sauce
| ½ t. sugar
| 1 t. black vinegar
| ¼ c. water

🐟   🐟   🐟

*1 lb. (450g) pez comestible o
  merluza
½ tz. albahaca fresca (Fig. 1)*

1 | *½ c. sal
| 1 C. vino para cocinar*

2 | *6 secciones de cebollín, 1¼"
| (3cm) de largo
| 1 C. raíz de jengibre rallada*

3 | *2 C. salsa de soya
| ½ c. azúcar
| 1 c. vinagre negro
| ¼ tz. agua*

1 魚以 **1** 料醃10分鐘，拭乾。

2 油3大匙燒熱，以中火將魚煎約4分鐘至兩面呈金黃色鏟至鍋邊，餘油炒香 **2** 料，再將魚置鍋中央，隨入 **3** 料以小火煮滾3分鐘，續入九層塔略拌即可。

☐ 魚肉質嫩，故一燒熟即可起鍋，以保持肉質鮮美。

🐟   🐟   🐟

1 Marinate fish in **1** for 10 minutes; pat dry.

2 Heat 3 T. oil; pan-fry fish over medium heat until golden on both sides, about 4 minutes; spatula to the side of wok; stir-fry **2** with remaining oil until fragrant; spatula fish to the center; add **3** ; cook over low heat for 3 minutes; mix with basil briefly; serve.

☐ The fish meat is very tender. To keep fish tasty, remove from heat immediately once it is done.

🐟   🐟   🐟

1 *Marine el pescado en **1** por 10 minutos; seque ligeramente.*

2 *Caliente 3 C. de aceite; fría el pescado en una sartén a fuego moderado hasta que esté dorado por ambos lados, como 4 minutos; muévalo a un lado de la sartén; fría revolviendo **2** con el aceite restante hasta que esté aromático; regrese el pescado al centro de la sartén; agregue **3** ; cocine a fuego lento por 3 minutos; mezcle con albahaca brevemente; sirva.*

☐ *La carne de pescado es muy tierna. Para mantener su sabroso sabor, saque del fuego inmediatamente después de cocido.*

1

67

蒜燒海鰻
Sea Eel in Garlic Sauce
Anguila de Mar en Salsa de Ajo

海鰻魚肉 .... 300公克（8兩）
燙熟白菜 .... 225公克（6兩）

1
鹽 .... ¼小匙
太白粉 1大匙

2
蒜（稍拍）................... 10粒
紅辣椒（切片）.............. 1條

3
酒 1大匙
醬油 2大匙
糖、麻油 各1小匙
水 .... ½杯

☙　　☙　　☙

⅔ lb.(300g) sea eel fillet
½ lb.(225g) cooked napa
　cabbage

1
¼ t. salt
1 T. cornstarch

2
10 garlic cloves, coarsely
　crushed
1 red chili pepper, sliced

3
1 T. cooking wine
2 T. soy sauce
1 t. ea.: sugar, sesame oil
½ c. water

☙　　☙　　☙

⅔ lb. (300g) filete de anguila
　de mar
½ lb. (225g) repollo napa
　cocido

1
¼ c. sal
1 C. maicena

2
10 dientes de ajo machacados
1 chile rojo, rebanado

3
1 C. vino para cocinar
2 C. salsa de soya
1 c. c/u: azúcar, aceite de
　sésamo
½ tz. agua

1 鰻魚肉切2公分×2公分×5公分之長方塊，調 **1** 料備用。

2 油4大匙燒熱，入鰻魚以中火煎至兩面呈金黃色取出，餘油炒香 **2** 料，隨入 **3** 料及魚塊煮約5分鐘至汁將收乾盛盤，以燙熟白菜墊底或圍邊即可。

☙　　☙　　☙

1 Cut eel fillet into ¾" × ¾" × 2" (2cm × 2cm × 5cm) long pieces; mix **1** well; set aside.

2 Heat 4 T. oil; pan-fry eel over medium heat until golden on both sides; remove. Stir-fry **2** with remaining oil until fragrant; add **3** and return pan-fried eel; cook until juice evaporates, about 5 minutes. Arrange the cabbage under or around eel.

☙　　☙　　☙

1 *Corte el filete de anguila en pedazos de ¾"×¾"×2" (2cm×2cm×5cm); mezcle* **1** *bien; deje aparte.*

2 *Caliente 4 C. de aceite; fría la anguila a fuego moderado hasta que esté dorada por ambos lados; retire. Fría-revolviendo* **2** *con el aceite restante hasta que esté aromático; agregue* **3** *y regrese el anguila frita; cocine hasta que el jugo se evapore, como 5 minutos. Acomode el repollo debajo o alrededor de la anguila.*

蜜汁海鰻　Glazed Sea Eel

Anguila de Mar Acaramelada

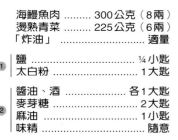

海鰻魚肉 .... 300公克（8兩）
燙熟青菜 .... 225公克（6兩）
「炸油」 .... 適量

1
鹽 .... ¼小匙
太白粉 1大匙

2
醬油、酒 各1大匙
麥芽糖 2大匙
麻油 1小匙
味精 .... 隨意

⅔ lb.(300g) sea eel fillet
½ lb.(225g) cooked green
   leafy vegetable
oil for deep-frying

1
¼ t. salt
1 T. cornstarch

2
1 T. ea.: soy sauce,
   cooking wine
2 T. maltose
1 t. sesame oil

⅔ lb. (300g) filete de anguila
   de mar
½ lb. (225g) vegetal de hojas
   verdes cocido
aceite para freír

1
¼ c. sal
1 C. maicena

2
1 C. c/u: salsa de soya, vino
   para cocinar
2 C. maltosa
1 c. aceite de sésamo

1 鰻魚肉切大丁，醃 **1** 料備用。

2 「炸油」燒熱，入鰻魚以中火炸至金黃色取出。將 **2** 料攪拌煮滾，隨入鰻魚炒拌至汁收乾盛盤，以燙熟青菜墊底或圍邊即可。

☐ 麥芽糖可用蜂蜜取代。

1 Cut eel fillet into large equal size pieces; marinate in **1** ; set aside.

2 Heat oil for deep-frying; deep-fry eel over medium heat until golden; remove. Stir and bring **2** to boil; return pan-fried eel; stir until juice evaporates; transfer to a serving plate. Arrange the green vegetable around or under the eel.

☐ Honey may be substituted for maltose.

1 *Corte el filete en pedazos largos del mismo tamaño; marine en* **1** *; deje aparte.*

2 *Caliente bastante aceite para freír; fría la anguila en una sartén a fuego moderado hasta que se dore; retire. Revuelva* **2** *y haga hervir; regrese la anguila frita a la sartén; revuelva hasta que el jugo se evapore; vacíe en el plato a servir. Acomode el vegetal verde debajo o alrededor de la anguila.*

☐ *Maltosa se puede substituir por miel.*

紅燒魚

Fish in Soy Sauce

Pescado en Salsa de Soya

4人份 · serves 4
4 porciones

魚 .... 600公克（1斤）

① 酒 1大匙
　 鹽 .... ½小匙

② 蔥段（8公分長）........... ½杯
　 薑絲 2大匙
　 辣椒（直剖4長條）.......... 1條

③ 水 4大匙
　 醬油 3大匙
　 酒 2大匙
　 糖 .... ½大匙
　 醋 1小匙

🍃　🍃　🍃

1⅓ lbs. (600g) fish

① **1 T. cooking wine, ½ t. salt**

② **½ c. green onion sections,
　 3" (8cm) long
2 T. shredded ginger root
1 chili pepper, cut
　 lengthwise into 4 strips**

③ **4 T. water, 3 T. soy sauce
2 T. cooking wine
½ T. sugar
1 t. vinegar**

🍃　🍃　🍃

1⅓ lbs. (600g) pescado

① *1 C. vino para cocinar, ½ c. sal*

② *½ tz. secciones de cebollín, 3"
　 (8cm) de largo
2 C. raíz de jengibre rallada
1 chile rojo, cortado a lo largo
　 en 4 tiras*

③ *4 C. agua, 3 C. salsa de soya
2 C. vino para cocinar
½ C. azúcar
1 c. vinagre*

1 魚於肉厚處劃刀痕（圖1），加 ① 料醃10分鐘拭乾。

2 油3大匙燒熱，放入魚以中火煎香至兩面呈金黃色鏟出，隨將 ② 料炒香，再入魚及 ③ 料煮開後翻面再煮約2分鐘即可。

🍃　🍃　🍃

1 Score fish in thick areas (Fig. 1); marinate in ① for 10 minutes; remove and pat dry.

2 Heat 3 T. oil; pan-fry fish over medium heat until golden on both sides; remove. Stir-fry ② until fragrant; return the pan-fried fish and ③; bring to boil. Turn the fish over and cook 2 minutes.

🍃　🍃　🍃

1 *Haga cortes en las áreas gruesas del pescado (Fig. 1); marine en ① por 10 minutos; retire y seque ligeramente.*

2 *Caliente 3 C. de aceite; fría el pescado en una sartén a fuego moderado hasta que esté dorado por ambos lados; retire. Fría-revolviendo ② hasta que esté aromático; regrese el pescado frito y ③; haga hervir. Voltee el pescado y cueza por 2 minutos.*

1

粉絲魚煲　Fish & Bean Thread Casserole

Guiso de Pescado y Brotes de Frijol

魚1條或取中段450公克（12兩）

1. 鹽 .... ¼小匙，酒 1大匙
2. 蒜末 2大匙
   薑絲 1大匙
3. 沙茶醬 2大匙
   麻油、糖 各1小匙
   醬油 ...... 1大匙，水 1½杯
4. 粉絲（圖1）...... 1把（30公克）
   紅蘿蔔絲 .... ¼杯
   金針菇 .... 115公克（3兩）

🐚　🐚　🐚

1 whole fish or middle
section, 1 lb. (450g)

1. ¼ t. salt, 1 T. cooking wine
2. 2 T. minced garlic cloves
   1 T. shredded ginger root
3. 2 T. barbecue sauce (sa-tsa)
   1 t. ea.: sesame oil, sugar
   1 T. soy sauce, 1½ c. water
4. 1 bunch bean threads,
   1 oz. (30g), Fig.1
   ¼ c. shredded carrots
   ¼ lb.(115g) golden
   mushrooms

🐚　🐚　🐚

*1 pescado entero o la sección
del medio, 1 lb. (450g)*

1. *¼ c. sal, 1 C. vino para cocinar*
2. *2 C. dientes de ajo finamente
   picados
   1 C. raíz de jengibre rallada*
3. *2 C. salsa de barbacoa (sa-tsa)
   1 c. c/u: aceite de sésamo,
   azúcar
   1 C. salsa de soya, 1½ tz. agua*
4. *1 manojo de brotes de frijol,
   1 oz. (30g), Fig. 1
   ¼ tz. zanahoria rallada
   ¼ lb. (115g) hongos dorados*

1

1 魚抹 ① 料醃10分鐘，粉絲泡軟切段。油3大匙燒熱，將魚煎至兩面呈金黃色取出，置砂鍋中。

2 熱油1大匙，爆香 ② 料，隨入 ③ 料煮滾倒於砂鍋中蓋鍋，以中小火煮約8分鐘，再入 ④ 料續煮約3分鐘即可。

☐ 本菜傳統是採用鯉魚，但亦可以草魚、黃魚或魚頭替代。

🐚　🐚　🐚

1 Spread ① evenly over fish and marinate for 10 minutes. Soak bean threads until softened then cut into sections. Heat 3 T. oil; pan-fry fish until golden on both sides; remove; place in a casserole.

2 Heat 1 T. oil; stir-fry ② until fragrant; add ③ ; bring to boil; pour into the casserole. Cover and cook casserole over medium-low heat, about 8 minutes; add ④ ; continue cooking for 3 minutes; serve.

☐ Traditionally, carp is used for this recipe. However, grass carp, yellow croaker, or fish head may be substituted for carp.

🐚　🐚　🐚

1 *Unte ① sobre todo el pescado y marine por 10 minutos. Remoje los brotes de frijol hasta que se ablanden luego córtelos en secciones. Caliente 3 C. de aceite; fría el pescado hasta que esté dorado por ambos lados; retire; coloque en una cacerola.*

2 *Caliente 1 C. de aceite; fría-revolviendo ② hasta que esté aromático; agregue ③ ; haga hervir; vacíe en la cacerola. Tape y cueza el guiso a fuego moderado bajo, como 8 minutos; agregue ④ ; continúe cociendo por 3 minutos; sirva.*

☐ *Tradicionalmente, se usa carpa para esta receta. Sin embargo, roncador amarillo o cabeza de pescado se puede substituir por carpa.*

味噌燒魚 　　　　　　Fish & Miso Sauce

Pescado en Salsa Miso

魚 .... 600公克（1斤）
蔥花 4大匙

① 味噌（圖1）.................... 3大匙
酒 2大匙
醬油 1大匙
糖 .... ½大匙
水 1杯

❧　　❧　　❧

1⅓ lbs. (600g) fish
4 T. chopped green onion

3 T. miso (Fig.1)
2 T. cooking wine
① 1 T. soy sauce
½ T. sugar
1 c. water

❧　　❧　　❧

1⅓ lbs. (600g) pescado
4 C. cebollín picado

3 C. miso (Fig. 1)
2 C. vino para cocinar
① 1 C. salsa de soya
½ C. azúcar
1 tz. agua

■　魚洗淨拭乾。油3大匙燒熱，大火將魚兩面煎成金黃色後隨入調勻的 ① 料蓋鍋，待燒開後改小火燒煮8分鐘（煮時需翻面）至汁剩約⅓杯呈濃稠狀時，撒上蔥花及麻油½大匙即可。

☐　若無味噌可用黑豆瓣醬或甜麵醬代替。

❧　　❧　　❧

■ Clean the fish; pat dry. Heat 3 T. oil; pan-fry fish over high heat until golden; add mixture ① ; cover and bring to boil; reduce heat to low; cook about 8 minutes until juice thickens and is reduced to about ⅓ c. (turn the fish over during cooking). Sprinkle with green onions and ½ T. sesame oil.

☐ Black bean paste or sweet bean paste may be substituted for miso, if miso is unavailable.

❧　　❧　　❧

■ *Lave el pescado; seque ligeramente. Caliente 3 C. de aceite; fría el pescado en una sartén a fuego alto hasta que se dore; agregue la mezcla ① ; tape y haga hervir; reduzca el fuego a lento; cueza como 8 minutos hasta que el jugo se espese y se reduzca como a ⅓ tz. (voltee el pescado mientras se cocina). Rocíe con los cebollines y con ½ C. aceite de sésamo.*

☐ *Se puede substituir pasta de frijol negro o pasta de frijol dulce por miso, si no puede encontrar miso.*

1

香醋燒魚　　Fish & Black Vinegar
Pescado en Vinagre Negro

魚 .... 600公克（1斤）
太白粉 2大匙
絞肉 .... 75公克（2兩）
蔥花 2大匙

① 酒 ...... 1大匙，鹽 .... ½小匙

② 蔥花 3大匙
　 薑、蒜末、辣豆瓣醬　各½大匙

③ 水 ...... 1¼杯，糖 1⅓大匙
　 醬油、黑醋 各2大匙
　 酒 .... 1大匙，麻油 ..... ½大匙

④ 太白粉 .... 1小匙，水 1大匙

❧　　❧　　❧

1⅓ lbs. (600g) fish
2 T. cornstarch
2½ oz.(75g) ground meat
2 T. chopped green onion

① 1 T. cooking wine, ½ t. salt

② 3 T. chopped green onion
　 ½ T. ea.(minced): ginger
　　 root, garlic cloves
　 ½ T. chili bean paste

③ 1¼ c. water, 1⅓ T. sugar
　 2 T. ea.: soy sauce, black
　　 vinegar
　 1 T. cooking wine
　 ½ T. sesame oil

④ 1 t. cornstarch, 1 T. water

❧　　❧　　❧

1⅓ lbs. (600g) pescado
2 C. maicena
2½ oz. (75g) carne molida
2 C. cebollín picado

① 1 C. vino para cocinar, ½ c. sal

② 3 C. cebollín picado
　 ½ C. c/u, (finamente picado):
　　 raíz de jengibre, dientes de ajo
　 ½ C. pasta de frijol picante

③ 1¼ tz. agua, 1⅓ C. azúcar
　 2 C. c/u: salsa de soya, vinagre negro
　 1 C. vino para cocinar
　 ½ C. aceite de sésamo

④ 1 c. maicena, 1 C. agua

1

1️⃣ 魚於肉厚處劃刀痕，加 ① 料醃15分鐘後拭乾，沾上太白粉。油3大匙燒熱，將魚煎至兩面呈金黃色時鏟出。

2️⃣ 油2大匙燒熱，炒香絞肉隨入 ② 料略炒（圖1），續加 ③ 料及魚煮5分鐘（煮時需翻面）至汁剩約一半時將魚鏟出，餘汁以 ④ 料勾芡淋在魚上並撒蔥花即成。

❧　　❧　　❧

1️⃣ Score fish in thick areas; marinate in ① for 15 minutes; remove and pat dry; coat with cornstarch. Heat 3 T. oil; pan-fry fish until golden on both sides; remove.

2️⃣ Heat 2 T. oil; stir-fry ground meat until fragrant; stir in ② briefly (Fig. 1), add ③ and return fish; cook until juice reduces to half (turn fish during cooking), 5 minutes; remove the fish. Add mixture ④ to thicken the remaining juice; pour over fish; sprinkle with green onions.

❧　　❧　　❧

1️⃣ *Haga cortes en las áreas gruesas del pescado; marine en ① por 15 minutos; retire y seque ligeramente; cubra con maicena. Caliente 3 C. de aceite; fría el pescado en una sartén hasta que esté dorado por ambos lados; retire.*

2️⃣ *Caliente 2 C. de aceite; fría-revolviendo la carne molida hasta que esté aromática; agregue ② revolviendo brevemente (Fig. 1), agregue ③ y regrese el pescado; cueza hasta que el jugo se reduzca a la mitad (voltee el pescado mientras se cocina), 5 minutos; retire el pescado. Agregue la mezcla ④ para espesar el jugo restante; vacíe sobre el pescado; espolvoree con cebollines.*

紅燒魚頭(一)　Fish Head in Soy Sauce (I)

Cabeza de Pescado en Salsa de Soya (I)

大魚頭 .... 600公克（1斤）
醬油 1大匙

① 蒜 12粒
　 蔥段（3公分長）............... 12段
　 紅辣椒（切段）................... 1條

② 醬油、酒 各3大匙
　 醋、糖、麻油 各1大匙
　 味精 .... 少許
　 水 .... 1¼ 杯

③ 太白粉 .... ½ 大匙，水 1大匙

1⅓ lbs. (600g) large fish
head
1 T. soy sauce

① 12 garlic cloves
12 sections green onions,
1¼" (3cm)
1 red chili pepper, cut into
sections

② 3 T. ea.: soy sauce,
cooking wine
1 T. ea.: vinegar, sugar,
sesame oil
1¼ c. stock

③ ½ T. cornstarch, 1 T. water

1⅓ lbs. (600g) cabeza grande
de pescado
1 C. salsa de soya

① 12 dientes de ajo
12 secciones de cebollín, 1¼"
(3cm)
1 chile rojo, cortado en
secciones

② 3 C. c/u: salsa de soya, vino
para cocinar
1 C. c/u: vinagre, azúcar,
aceite de sésamo
1¼ tz. caldo

③ ½ C. maicena, 1 C. agua

① 魚頭洗淨於肉厚處劃刀痕，加醬油抹勻醃10分鐘，煎前拭乾。油3大匙燒熱，將魚頭兩面煎呈金黃色。

② 油3大匙燒熱，炒香 ① 料，隨入魚頭及 ② 料大火燒開後蓋鍋改小火燜煮10分鐘（煮時需翻面）至汁剩約一半時用拌勻的 ③ 料勾芡即成。

紅燒魚頭 (二) 將魚頭剁塊同法燒煮，② 料內的水改為1杯，燜煮時間縮短為5分鐘。

① Clean fish head. Score head in thick fleshy areas. Spread soy sauce evenly over the fish and marinate for 10 minutes; pat dry before pan-frying. Heat 3 T. oil; pan-fry fish head until golden on both sides; remove.

② Heat 3 T. oil; stir-fry ① until fragrant; return head and add ② ; bring to boil over high heat; reduce heat to low; cover and simmer until juice reduces to half (turn fish during cooking), 10 minutes; add mixture ③ to thicken the juice; serve.

Fish Head in Soy Sauce (II) Cut fish head in pieces. Use the above ingredients and procedures. Reduce the water in ingredient ② to 1 c. Shorten the simmering time of step ② to 5 minutes.

① *Limpie la cabeza. Haga cortes en las áreas gruesas y carnosas. Unte salsa de soya por parejo sobre el pescado y marine por 10 minutos; seque ligeramente antes de freír. Caliente 3 C. de aceite; fría la cabeza en la sartén hasta que esté dorada por ambos lados; retire,*

② *Caliente 3 C. de aceite; fría-revolviendo ① hasta que esté aromático; regrese la cabeza y agregue ② ; haga hervir a fuego alto; baje el fuego a lento; tape y cocine a fuego lento hasta que el jugo se haya reducido a la mitad (voltee el pescado mientras se cocina), 10 minutos; agregue la mezcla ③ para espesar el jugo; sirva.*

Cabeza de Pescado en Salsa de Soya (II) *Corte la cabeza de pescado en pedazos. Use los ingredientes y siga los procedimientos de arriba. Reduzca el agua en los ingredientes de ② a 1 tz. Reduzca el tiempo que se cocina a fuego lento del paso ② a 5 minutos.*

紅燒魚頭 (二) · Fish Head in Soy Sauce (II)
Cabeza de Pescado en Salsa de Soya (II)

魚頭燒白菜　Stewed Fish Head & Cabbage

Estofado de Cabeza de Pescado con Repollo

大魚頭 .... 600公克（1斤）
大白菜（切大塊）1200公克（2斤）

① 醬油 1½大匙
酒 .... ½大匙

② 醬油 1½大匙
鹽 1½小匙
高湯 1½杯

1⅓ lbs. (600g) large fish head
2⅔ lbs. (1200g) nappa cabbage (cut in large pieces)

① 1½ T. soy sauce
½ T. cooking wine

② 1½ T. soy sauce
1½ t. salt
1½ c. stock

1⅓ lbs. (600g) cabeza grande de pescado
2⅔ lbs. (1200g) repollo napa (cortado en pedazos grandes)

① *1½ C. salsa de soya*
½ C. vino para cocinar

② *1½ C. salsa de soya*
1½ c. sal
1½ tz. caldo

1 魚頭洗淨於肉厚處劃刀痕，加 ① 料抹勻醃10分鐘，煎前拭乾。

2 油3大匙燒熱，將魚頭兩面煎成金黃色。

3 油3大匙燒熱，放入大白菜炒軟後移入砂鍋或深鍋內，魚頭置於中間，加入 ② 料以小火燜煮40分鐘即可。

1 Clean the fish head; score head in thick areas; spread ① evenly over the fish and marinate for 10 minutes; pat dry before pan-frying.

2 Heat 3 T. oil; pan-fry fish head until golden on both sides.

3 Heat 3 T. oil; stir-fry nappa cabbage until softened; transfer the cabbage to a casserole or a deep pan; place fish in the center of casserole. Add ② to casserole; stew over low heat for 40 minutes.

1 *Limpie la cabeza; haga cortes en las áreas gruesas; unte ① por parejo sobre el pescado y marine por 10 minutos; seque ligeramente antes de freír.*

2 *Caliente 3 C. de aceite; fría la cabeza en una sartén hasta que esté dorada por ambos lados.*

3 *Caliente 3 C. de aceite; fría-revolviendo el repollo napa hasta que se ablande; vacíe el repollo a una cacerola o una cazuela honda; coloque la cabeza en el centro de la cacerola. Agregue ② a la cacerola; cocine el estofado a fuego lento por 40 minutos.*

紅燒扣鰻
Steamed Eel & Soy Sauce

宴客菜 · *Serve at a formal meal*

河鰻 .... 900公克（1斤8兩）
太白粉 1½大匙
「炸油」 .... 適量
蒜粒 .... ½杯
青江菜（切半） 6棵

① 醬油 3大匙
麻油 .... ½大匙
酒、糖 各1大匙
水 .... ½杯
味精、胡椒、醋 .... 各少許

② 太白粉 .... ½大匙
水 1大匙

2 lbs. (900g) river eel
1½ T. cornstarch
oil for deep-frying
½ c. garlic cloves
6 bok choy (cut lengthwise
   in half)

① 3 T. soy sauce
½ T. sesame oil
1 T. ea.: cooking wine,
   sugar
½ c. water
dash of ea.: pepper, vinegar

② ½ T. cornstarch, 1 T. water

1 河鰻處理乾淨（見89頁枸杞燉鰻），切3公分長段，加太白粉拌勻。炸油燒熱，將鰻魚炸呈金黃色（約2分鐘）撈出，將蒜粒亦炸呈金黃色備用。

2 將炸好的鰻魚切口朝下整齊排列在蒸碗內，再放入蒜粒及 ① 料蒸40分鐘取出，倒出湯汁，湯汁用拌勻的 ② 料勾成薄汁。

3 鰻魚倒扣在盤內，用燙熟的青江菜圍邊，再淋上鰻魚汁即成。

1 Clean eel (see "Steamed Eel & Boxphorn Fruit", p. 89); cut into 1¼" (3cm) sections; coat evenly with cornstarch. Heat oil deep-fry eel 2 minutes until golden; remove. Deep-fry garlic cloves until golden.

2 Arrange the fried eel, cut side down, on a heatproof bowl; add garlic and ① ; steam the eel for 40 minutes; remove the bowl from heat. Pour the liquid in the bowl into a saucepan; thicken with mixture ② .

3 Invert the heatproof bowl onto a serving bowl. Blanch and arrange bok choy around the eel. Pour thickened liquid over the eel and bok choy.

Anguila con Salsa de Soya al Vapor

Fotos a la izq.

Se sirve en una cena formal

2 lbs. (900g) anguila de río
1½ C. maicena
aceite para freír
½ tz. dientes de ajo
6 bok choy (cortados a lo largo
*   por la mitad)*

①
3 C. salsa de soya
½ C. aceite de sésamo
1 C. c/u: vino para cocinar,
*   azúcar*
½ tz. agua
pizca de pimienta
gotas de vinagre

② *½ C. maicena, 1 C. agua*

1 *Limpie la anguila (vea "Anguila y Fruta Seca al Vapor", p. 89); corte en secciones de 1¼" (3cm) de largo; reboce completamente con maicena. Caliente bastante aceite para freír; fría la anguila hasta que se dore, como 2 minutos; retire. Fría los dientes de ajo hasta que se doren; deje aparte.*

2 *Acomode la anguila frita, la parte donde se cortó boca abajo, en un tazón resistente al calor; agregue el ajo y* **①** *; cocine la anguila al vapor por 40 minutos; retire el tazón del fuego. Vacíe el líquido del tazón a una cacerola; espese con la mezcla* **②** *.*

3 *Voltee el tazón sobre el plato a servir. Sumerja el bok choy en agua hirviendo y acomode alrededor de la anguila. Vacíe el líquido espesado sobre la anguila y bok choy.*

紅燒鰻魚 — Eel in Soy Sauce

Anguila en Salsa de Soya

宴客菜 · *Serve at a formal meal*

Se sirve en una cena formal

參照「紅燒扣鰻」（見76頁），將青江菜改為香菇6朵（泡軟、切半），**①** 料內之水改為2杯，其它材料同。另蔥6段、薑6片備用。

🍃   🍃   🍃

6 green onion sections,
**   1¼" (3cm)**
6 slices ginger root
Other ingredients are the
**   same as "Steamed Eel &**
**   Soy Sauce," p. 76, except**
**   substitute bok choy with 6**
**   Chinese black mushrooms**
**   and increase the water in**
**   ingredients ① to 2 c.**

🍃   🍃   🍃

6 secciones de cebollín, 1¼" (3cm)
6 rebanadas raíz de jengibre
Los demás ingredientes son como
*   para "Anguila con Salsa de*
*   Soya al Vapor," p. 76, excepto*
*   substituya el bok choy por 6*
*   hongos chinos negros y aumente*
*   el agua en los ingredientes de*
*   ① a 2 tz.*

1 參照紅燒扣鰻做法 **1** ，將鰻魚改切4公分長段。

2 油3大匙燒熱，炒香蔥、薑，隨入 **①** 料、蒜粒、鰻魚、香菇等，蓋鍋燜煮20分鐘至汁約剩⅓時，以 **②** 料勾茨即可。

🍃   🍃   🍃

1 Follow the same procedure as Steamed Eel & Soy Sauce in Step **1** (cut eel into 1½" or 4cm long sections).

2 Heat 3 T. oil; stir-fry green onion and ginger root until fragrant; add **①** , garlic cloves, eel, and Chinese black mushrooms; cover and cook until liquid reduces to ⅓, 20 minutes; add **②** to thicken; serve.

🍃   🍃   🍃

1 *Siga los mismos procedimientos de Anguila con Salsa de Soya al Vapor en paso* **1** *(corte la anguila en secciones de 1½" ó 4cm de largo).*

2 *Caliente 3 C. de aceite; fría-revolviendo el cebollín y raíz de jengibre hasta que esté aromático; agregue* **①** *, los dientes de ajo, la anguila, y los hongos negros chinos; tape y cueza hasta que el líquido se reduzca a ⅓, 20 minutos; agregue* **②** *para espesar; sirva.*

紅燒魚唇　Shark's Lips in Soy Sauce

Labios de Tiburón en Salsa de Soya

宴客菜 · Serve at a formal meal
Se sirve en una cena formal

水發魚唇或厚魚皮600公克(1斤)
豌豆夾 12片

① | 蔥 .... 2支，薑 2片
　 | 酒 .... 2大匙，水 3杯

② | 蔥 .... 6小段，薑 6片
　 | 辣椒片..1條，蒜（拍破）..2粒

③ | 香菇片 .... 4朵，洋菇 12個
　 | 筍、瘦肉 各12片

④ | 高湯 .... 1 ½ 杯
　 | 酒、醬油 各2大匙
　 | 麻油、黑醋 各1大匙
　 | 糖 .... ½ 大匙，鹽 ..... ½ 小匙

⑤ | 太白粉 ... 1大匙，水 2大匙

ᴥ　　ᴥ　　ᴥ

1⅓ lbs. (600g) presoftened
　 shark's lips or thick fish skin
12 Chinese snow peas

① | 2 green onions
　 | 2 slices ginger root
　 | 2 T. cooking wine, 3c. water

② | 6 small green onion sections
　 | 6 slices ginger root
　 | 1 sliced red chili pepper
　 | 2 garlic cloves, crushed

③ | 4 sliced Chinese black mushrooms
　 | 12 mushrooms
　 | 12 slices ea.: bamboo shoots,
　 | 　lean meat

④ | 2 T. ea.: cooking wine, soy sauce
　 | 1 T. ea.: sesame oil, black vinegar
　 | ½ T. sugar, ½ t. salt, 1½ c. stock

⑤ | 1 T. cornstarch, 2 T. water

ᴥ　　ᴥ　　ᴥ

1⅓ lbs. (600g) labios de tiburón
　 ablandados o piel gruesa de
　 pescado
12 chícharos chinos

① | *2 cebollines*
　 | *2 rebanadas de raíz de jengibre*
　 | *2 C. vino para cocinar, 3 tz. agua*

② | *6 secciones pequeñas de cebollín*
　 | *6 rebanadas raíz de jengibre*
　 | *1 chile rojo rebanado*
　 | *2 dientes de ajo machacados*

③ | *4 hongos chinos negros rebanados*
　 | *12 hongos*
　 | *12 rebanadas c/u: brotes de bambú,*
　 | *carne magra*

④ | *2 C. c/u: vino para cocinar, salsa de*
　 | *soya*
　 | *1 C. c/u: aceite de sésamo, vinagre*
　 | *negro*
　 | *½ C. azúcar, ½ c. sal, 1½ tz. caldo*

⑤ | *1 C. maicena, 2 C. agua*

1

① 將魚唇殘留的魚肉剔除洗淨，切大塊，① 料燒開入魚唇煮5分鐘撈出瀝乾。

② 油3大匙燒熱，炒香 ② 料隨入 ③ 料略炒，續加 ④ 料及魚唇，蓋鍋用中火燒煮8分鐘至汁剩一半時，放入豌豆莢並加 ⑤ 料勾成薄汁即成。

紅燒魚肚　參照「紅燒魚唇」做法，將魚唇改用炸魚肚，其他材料均同。
炸魚肚：乾魚肚（圖1）浸泡在油內隔夜，再用小火炸至魚肚脹大浮起。

ᴥ　　ᴥ　　ᴥ

1 Remove remaining meat left around the shark's lips; clean; cut into large pieces. Bring ① to boil, cook shark's lips for 5 minutes; remove and drain.

2 Heat 3 T. oil; stir-fry ② until fragrant; stir in ③ briefly; add ④ and shark's lips; cover and cook over medium heat until juice reduces to half, 8 minutes; add Chinese snow peas then ⑤ to thicken the mixture; serve.

Fish Bellies in Soy Sauce Follow the same procedure as above. Substitute fried fish bellies for fish lips; other ingredients are the same as above. To fry fish bellies, soak dried fish bellies (Fig. 1) in oil overnight then deep-fry over low heat until expanded and floating.

ᴥ　　ᴥ　　ᴥ

1 *Quite cualquier carne restante a los labios de tiburón; limpie; corte en pedazos grandes. Haga hervir ①, cocine los labios de tiburón por 5 minutos; retire y escurra.*

2 *Caliente 3 C. de aceite; fría-revolviendo ② hasta que esté aromático; agregue ③ revolviendo brevemente; agregue ④ y los labios de tiburón; tape y cueza a fuego moderado hasta que el jugo se reduzca a la mitad, 8 minutos; agregue los chícharos luego ⑤ para espesar la mezcla; sirva.*

Pancitas de Pescado en Salsa de Soya *Siga los mismos procedimientos de arriba. Substituya los labios de tiburón por las pancitas de pescado; los otros ingredientes son como los de arriba. Para freír las pancitas de pescado, remoje las pancitas secas (Fig. 1) en aceite toda la noche luego fría a fuego bajo hasta que se expandan y floten.*

三絲魚翅 Shark's Fin & Assorted Vegetables

Aleta de Tiburón con Varios Vegetales 宴客菜 · *Serve at a formal meal*
Se sirve en una cena formal

發好魚翅 .... 225公克（6兩）
雞高湯 2杯

① 蔥.........6小段、薑 6片
酒 .... 1大匙，水 3杯

② 香菇絲 4大匙
蔥段 3支

肉絲 .... ½杯

③ 熟筍絲或金針菇 1杯
蠔油、醬油 .... 各½大匙
胡椒 .... ⅛小匙
鹽、酒、麻油 各1小匙
雞高湯 3杯

④ 太白粉 .... 3大匙，水 3大匙

❧ ❧ ❧

**½ lb.(225g) presoftened
shark's fin
2 c. chicken stock**

① **6 green onion sections
6 ginger root slices
1 T. cooking wine
3 c. water**

② **4 T. shredded Chinese
black mushrooms
3 green onions, sectioned**

½ c. shredded pork

③ **1 c. shredded & cooked
bamboo shoots or
golden mushrooms
½ T. ea.: oyster sauce, soy
sauce
⅛ t. pepper
1 t. ea.: salt, cooking wine,
sesame oil
3 c. chicken stock**

④ **3 T. cornstarch, 3 T. water**

❧ ❧ ❧

*½ lb. (225g) aleta de tiburón
ablandada
2 tz. caldo de pollo*

① *6 secciones de cebollín
6 rebanadas raíz de jengibre
1 C. vino para cocinar
3 tz. agua*

② *4 C. hongos chinos negros rallados
3 cebollines cortados en secciones*

½ tz. carne de cerdo desmenuzada

③ *1 tz. brotes de bambú cocidos,
rallados u hongos dorados
½ C. c/u: salsa de ostiones,
salsa de soya
⅛ c. pimienta
1 c. c/u: sal, vino para cocinar,
aceite de sésamo
3 tz. caldo de pollo*

④ *3 C. maicena, 3 C. agua*

1 將 ① 料煮開，入魚翅川燙5分鐘撈起，加雞高湯入電鍋中蒸軟（約2小時）或煮滾入燜燒鍋燜軟備用。

2 油2大匙燒熱，炒香 ② 料，入肉絲炒開，隨加 ③ 料並倒入燜軟的魚翅煮滾，以拌勻的 ④ 料勾芡即可。食時可依喜好加上香菜、紅醋或黑醋等。

雞高湯 雞1200公克（2斤）入開水川燙撈起，加水10杯燒開後改小火煮2小時。

❧ ❧ ❧

1 Bring ① to boil; blanch shark's fin for 5 minutes; remove. Add chicken stock; steam in electric cooker until softened, about 2 hours, or cook in slow cooker until softened; set aside.

2 Heat 2 T. oil; stir-fry ② until fragrant; stir-fry shredded meat until separated; add ③ and softened shark's fin; bring to boil; add mixture ④; stir until thickened. Serve with coriander, red vinegar, or black vinegar, as desired.

Homemade Chicken Stock Bring water to boil; blanch 2⅔ lbs. (1200g) chicken; remove. Add 10 c. water; bring to boil; cook chicken over low heat for 2 hours.

❧ ❧ ❧

1 *Haga hervir ①; sumerja la aleta de tiburón por 5 minutos; retire. Agregue el caldo de pollo; cocine al vapor en vaporera eléctrica hasta que se ablande, como 2 horas, o cocine en una olla donde se cocina despacio hasta que se ablande; deje aparte.*

2 *Caliente 2 C. de aceite; fría-revolviendo ② hasta que esté aromático; fría-revolviendo la carne desmenuzada hasta que se separe; agregue ③ y la aleta de tiburón ablandada; haga hervir; agregue la mezcla ④; revuelva hasta que espese. Sirva con cilantro, vinagre rojo, o vinagre negro, al gusto.*

Caldo de Pollo Hecho en Casa *Haga hervir agua; sumerja 2⅔ lbs. (1200g) de pollo; retire. Agregue 10 tz. agua; haga hervir, cocine el pollo a fuego lento por 2 horas.*

紅燒甲魚   Turtle in Soy Sauce

Tortuga en Salsa de Soya

宴客菜 · *Serve at a formal meal*
Se sirve en una cena formal

甲魚 1隻
　約1斤半-2斤（900-1200公克）
雞翅（中段） 12隻
香菇（泡軟切半） 6朵
筍 12片

① 蔥 6小段
　薑 6片
　蒜（拍破） 6粒

② 高湯 3杯
　酒、醬油 各4大匙
　糖、麻油 .... 各½大匙
　味精、胡椒 .... 各少許

③ 太白粉 .... 2小匙，水 2大匙

❧　　❧　　❧

**1 green turtle, 2 lbs.-2⅔ lbs.
(900g-1200g)
12 chicken wings (middle
part)
6 chinese black marshrooms
(presoftened cut in half)
12 bamboo shoot slices**

① **6 green onion sections
6 ginger root slices
6 crushed garlic cloves**

② **3 c. stock
4 T.ea.: cooking wine, soy
sauce
½ T.ea.: sugar, sesame oil
dash of pepper**

③ **2 t. cornstarch, 2 T. water**

❧　　❧　　❧

*1 tortuga verde, 2 lbs.-2⅔ lbs.
(900g-1200g)
12 alas de pollo (parte del
centro)
6 hongos chinos negros
(remojados y cortados por la
mitad)
12 brotes de bambú*

① *6 secciones de cebollín
6 rebanadas raíz de jengibre
6 dientes de ajo, machacados*

② *3 tz. caldo
4 C. c/u: vino para cocinar,
salsa de soya
½ C. c/u: azúcar, aceite de
sésamo
pizca de pimienta*

③ *2 c. maicena, 2 C. agua*

1 甲魚切大塊，與雞翅一起拌入醬油1大匙。炸油燒熱，將甲魚及雞翅分別炸約3分鐘呈金黃色撈出。

2 油3大匙炒香 ① 料並加香菇及筍略炒，隨入 ② 料、甲魚及雞翅，煮開後蓋鍋改小火續煮約40分鐘至汁剩一半時，以拌勻的 ③ 料勾芡即成。

❧　　❧　　❧

1 Cut turtle into large pieces; marinate with chicken wings in 1 T. soy sauce. Heat oil for deep-frying; deep-fry turtle and chicken wings separately until golden, each about 3 minutes; remove.

2 Heat 3 T. oil; stir-fry ① until fragrant; stir in Chinese black mushrooms and bamboo shoots briefly; add ② ; return turtle and chicken wings to wok; bring to boil; reduce heat to low; cover and cook until juice reduces to half, about 40 minutes; thicken the juice with mixture ③ ; serve.

❧　　❧　　❧

1 *Corte la tortuga en pedazos grandes; marine con las alas de pollo en 1 C. de salsa de soya. Caliente bastante aceite para freír; fría la tortuga y las alas de pollo por separado hasta que estén doradas, como 3 minutos cada uno; retire.*

2 *Caliente 3 C. de aceite; fría-revolviendo ① hasta que esté aromático; agregue mezclando brevemente los hongos chinos negros y brotes de bambú; agregue ② ; devuelva la tortuga y el pollo a la sartén; haga hervir; baje el fuego a lento; cubra y cocine hasta que los jugos se reduzcan a la mitad, como 40 minutos; espese el jugo con la mezcla ③ ; sirva.*

生吃鱺魚 Raw Fish Salad

Ensalada de Pescado Crudo

宴客菜 · *Serve at a formal meal*

活鱺魚 .... 900公克（1斤8兩）
白蘿蔔絲 2杯
紅蘿蔔絲 .... ¼杯
圍邊用料：櫻桃、巴西利、生菜

① 綠或黃芥末醬 .... 適量
　　醬油 2大匙

2 lbs. (900g) live or fresh
　sea fish
2 c. shredded white radish
¼ c. shredded carrots
For garnish: cherries,
　parsley, lettuce

① mustard as desired
　2 T. soy sauce

2 lbs. (900g) pescado de mar
　vivo o fresco
2 tz. rábano blanco rallado
¼ tz. zanahoria rallada
Para adornar: cerezas, perejil,
　lechuga

① mostaza al gusto
　2 C. salsa de soya

1 活魚取肉切薄片（見第8頁），立刻放入冰水內（可加冰塊），輕攪拌約3分鐘，肉質轉白瀝乾（此稱水洗法，可使肉質爽脆，但一定要用活魚、活蝦等）。

2 白、紅蘿蔔絲泡水約10分鐘，撈出瀝乾鋪在盤上，上置魚片，沾 **①** 料食用。

□ 白蘿蔔絲：取白蘿蔔中段長約10公分，去皮修成圓筒狀，旋轉片出長條薄片（圖1），再將薄片捲成圓筒狀後切絲（圖2），或用刨子刨絲。

1 Fillet live or fresh fish; slice thinly (see p. 8); immediately drop into ice water (ice cubes can be added); stir gently about 3 minutes until the meat turns white; drain (this ice water cleaning method should only be used for live fish or shrimp to make them crisp).

2 Soak shredded white radish and carrots in water for 10 minutes; remove; drain; line a plate and top with fish slices; serve with **①** as a dip.

□ Shredded white radish: Use only the middle section of the white radish, about 4" (10cm) long; peel and shape to a cylinder; use of a spiral slicer turns radish into a thin, continuous curl (Fig. 1); reshape the long, spiral slice into a cylinder; shred (Fig. 2) with knife, or grate.

1 *Corte el pescado vivo o fresco en filetes; corte en rebanadas delgadas (vea p. 8); sumerja inmediatamente en agua helada (se puede agregar cubos de hielo); mezcle ligeramente como 3 minutos hasta que la carne se ponga blanca; escurra (solamente use este método con pescado vivo o camarones para hacerlos crujientes).*

2 *Remoje el rábano blanco rallado y zanahoria en agua por 10 minutos; retire; escurra; cubra un plato con el rábano y agregue encima las rebanadas de pescado; sirva con **①** como dip.*

□ *Rábano blanco rallado: Solamente use la parte del centro del rábano blanco; como 4" (10cm) de largo; pele en forma de cilindro; el uso de un rabanador espiral convierte el rábano en un rollo delgado y continuo (Fig. 1); vuelva a formar el pedazo largo y espiral en un cilindro; raspe (Fig. 2) con un cuchillo o con un rallador.*

1

2

砂鍋魚頭（一）　Fish Head Casserole Soup(I)

Guiso de Sopa de Cabeza de Pescado (I)

4人份・serves 4
4 porciones

大魚頭 .... 600公克（1斤）
豆腐（切塊）.... 300公克（8兩）

① 辣豆瓣醬 .... ½ 大匙
蔥 .... 6小段，薑 6片
蒜（拍破） 6粒

② 瘦肉（豬或雞）、筍 各12片
香菇（泡軟切半） 6朵

③ 醬油 5大匙
糖、麻油 各1大匙
醋.....1小匙，高湯 2杯

④ 太白粉、水 各1大匙

🐚　🐚　🐚

1 large fish head,
　　1⅓ lbs. (600g)
⅔ lb.(300g) bean curd, cut
　　in pieces

① ½ T. chili bean paste
6 green onion sections
6 ginger root slices
6 garlic cloves, coarsely
　　crushed

② 12 slices ea.: lean meat
　　(pork or chicken),
　　bamboo shoots
6 Chinese black mushrooms,
　　presoftened and cut in half

③ 5 T. soy sauce
1 T. ea.: sugar, sesame oil
1 t. vinegar, 2 c. stock

④ 1 T. cornstarch, 1 T. water

🐚　🐚　🐚

① *1 cabeza de pescado grande,*
　　1⅓ lbs. (600g)
⅔ lb. (300g) tofu, cortado en
　　pedazos

① *½ C. pasta de frijol picante*
6 secciones de cebollín
6 rebanadas raíz de jengibre
6 dientes de ajo, poco machacados

② *12 rebanadas, c/u: carne*
　　magra (puerco o pollo),
　　brotes de bambú
6 hongos chinos negros, ablandados
　　y cortados por la mitad

③ *5 C. salsa de soya*
1 C. c/u: azúcar, aceite de sésamo
1 c. vinagre, 2 tz. caldo

④ *1 C. maicena, 1 C. agua*

1️⃣ 魚頭洗淨由中間剁開成兩半（圖1），拭乾加醬油1大匙抹勻。煎前拭乾。

2️⃣ 油4大匙燒熱，將魚頭煎香並呈金黃色。

3️⃣ 油3大匙燒熱炒香 ① 料，隨入 ② 料略炒後與魚頭及 ③ 料移入砂鍋，煮開後改小火蓋鍋燜煮10分鐘，加入豆腐續煮4分鐘，再以 ④ 料勾芡即可趁熱食用。

🐚　🐚　🐚

1️⃣ Clean fish head; halve the head (Fig. 1); pat dry; spread 1 T. soy sauce thoroughly over the fish; pat dry before pan-frying.

2️⃣ Heat 4 T. oil; pan-fry fish head until fragrant and golden.

3️⃣ Heat 3 T. oil; stir-fry ① until fragrant; stir in ② briefly; transfer with fish head and ③ into a casserole; bring to boil; reduce heat to low; cover and simmer for 10 minutes; add bean curd; continue cooking for 4 minutes; thicken with mixture ④; serve hot.

🐚　🐚　🐚

1️⃣ *Limpie la cabeza de pescado; córtela por la mitad (Fig. 1); seque ligeramente; unte completamente 1 C. salsa de soya sobre el pescado; seque ligeramente antes de freír en la sartén.*

2️⃣ *Caliente 4 C. de aceite; fría la cabeza de pescado hasta que esté aromática y dorada.*

3️⃣ *Caliente 3 C. de aceite; fría-revolviendo ① hasta que esté aromático; agregue ② revolviendo brevemente; vacíe con la cabeza de pescado y ③ en una cacerola; haga hervir; reduzca el fuego a lento; tape y cocine lentamente por 10 minutos; agregue el tofu; continúe cocinando por 4 minutos; espese con la mezcla ④; sirva caliente.*

1

砂鍋魚頭(二) Fish Head Casserole Soup(II)

Guiso de Sopa de Cabeza de Pescado (II)

鰱魚頭 .... 600公克（約1斤）
太白粉 1大匙
豆腐2塊 .... 300公克（8兩）
蒜苗 1支
炸熟芋頭 1杯

① 辣豆瓣醬 .... ½大匙
　 蔥（3公分長） 6段
　 薑............3片，蒜 6粒

② 大白菜、金針菇、木耳、
　 魚板片 ..共450公克（12兩）

③ 醬油 ...... 2大匙，鹽 ... 1小匙
　 高湯 6杯
　 味精 .... 隨意

❧　　❧　　❧

1 silver carp head,
　 1⅓ lbs. (600g)
1 T. cornstarch
2 bean curd, ⅔ lb.(300g)
1 fresh garlic spear
1 c. deep-fried taro

① ½ T. chili bean paste
　 6 green onion sections,
　 1¼" (3cm) long
　 3 slices ginger root
　 6 garlic cloves

② 1 lb. (450g) total: nappa
　 cabbage, golden
　 mushrooms, dried wood
　 ears, sliced fish cake

③ 2 T. soy sauce, 1 t. salt
　 6 c. stock

❧　　❧　　❧

① *1 cabeza de carpa plateada,*
　 1⅓ lbs. (600g)
1 C. maicena
2 pedazos de tofu, ⅔ lb. (300g)
1 brote entero de ajo
1 tz. taro frito

① *½ C. pasta de frijol picante*
　 6 secciones de cebollín, 1¼"
　 (3cm) de largo
　 3 rebanadas raíz de jengibre
　 6 dientes de ajo

② *1 lb. (450g) en total: repollo*
　 napa, hongos dorados,
　 orejas de madera secas,
　 pasta de pescado en
　 rebanadas

③ *2 C. salsa de soya, 1 c. sal*
　 6 tz. caldo

1 魚頭於肉厚處劃刀，抹上太白粉，豆腐切塊。蒜苗和大白菜均切段備用。

2 油4大匙燒熱，將魚頭煎香並呈金黃色取出，餘油炒香 ① 料，加 ② 料略炒後與魚頭、豆腐、芋頭及 ③ 料移入砂鍋煮滾，改中火續煮約10分鐘後，入蒜苗一滾即可。

☐ 此道可與白飯配食，亦可邊煮邊食，即為簡易便餐。

❧　　❧　　❧

1 Score fish head in thick meat places; coat with cornstarch. Cut bean curd into pieces. Cut garlic and nappa cabbage into sections; set aside.

2 Heat 4 T. oil; pan-fry fish head until golden and fragrant; remove. Stir-fry ① with remaining oil until fragrant; stir in ② briefly; transfer with fish, bean curd, taro, and ③ to a casserole; bring to boil; reduce heat to medium; cook and simmer for 10 minutes; add garlic; bring to boil; serve.

☐ This dish goes well with rice. Can be cooked and served at the table. It also serves as a fast, simple, tasty, casual meal.

❧　　❧　　❧

1 *Haga cortes a la cabeza en las áreas carnosas gruesas; reboce con maicena. Corte el tofu en pedazos. Corte el brote de ajo y el repollo napa en secciones; deje aparte.*

2 *Caliente 4 C. de aceite; fría la cabeza de pescado hasta que esté aromática y dorada; retire. Fría-revolviendo ① con el aceite restante hasta que esté aromático; agregue ② revolviendo brevemente; vacíe con el pescado, el tofu, taro, y ③ a una cacerola; haga hervir; reduzca el fuego a moderado; cocine a fuego lento por 10 minutos; agregue el ajo; haga hervir; sirva.*

☐ *Este platillo se complementa con arroz. Se puede cocinar y servir en la mesa. Es adecuado también para una merienda rápida, simple y sabrosa.*

Sopa de Pescado con Jugo de Limón

檸檬 2片

① 鮮魚肉 .... 150公克（4兩）
蝦仁、金針菇　各75公克（2兩）
草菇或鮮香菇 .... 75公克（2兩）

② 水 5杯
鹽 1小匙
味精或鰹魚粉 .... ¼小匙
嫩薑絲 1大匙

2 lemon slices

① **⅓ lb.(150g) fish fillets**
2½ oz.(75g) ea.: shelled
shrimp, golden
mushrooms
2½ oz.(75g) straw
mushrooms or fresh
Chinese black
mushrooms

② **5 c. water**
1 t. salt
¼ t. dashi
1 T. shredded baby ginger
root

2 rebanadas de limón

① *⅓ lb. (150g) filetes de pescado*
2½ oz. (75g) c/u: camarón
pelado, hongos dorados
2½ oz. (75g) hongos con tallo u
hongos chinos negros,
frescos

② *5 tz. agua*
1 c. sal
¼ c. dashi
1 C. raíz de jengibre tierna
rallada

1　魚肉切0.5公分薄片，金針菇切除根部備用。

2　將 ② 料燒開，入 ① 料（亦可先川燙，湯汁較清）以大火燒開即刻熄火以保鮮嫩，擠入檸檬汁，並加少許貝芽菜趁熱食用。

□　檸檬汁具清香味，可去腥又富維他命C，非常適合用於魚類。

1　Cut fish into ¼" (0.5cm) thin slices; cut off the roots of golden mushrooms; set aside.

2　Bring ② to boil; add ① (or blanch ① before cooking to make soup clearer) and cook over high heat until boiling; turn off heat immediately to keep fish tender; sprinkle in lemon juice and a few bean sprouts; serve hot.

□　The fresh smelling lemon juice is a perfect match for the fish. It not only removes any offensive fish smell, but adds vitamin c to the food.

1　*Corte el pescado en rebanadas delgadas de ¼" (0.5cm); córtele las raíces a los hongos dorados; deje aparte.*

2　*Haga hervir ② ; agregue ① (o sumerja ① antes de cocinar en agua hirviendo para hacer una sopa más clara) y cueza a fuego alto hasta que hierva; apague el fuego inmediatamente para mantener tierno el pescado; rocíe con jugo de limón y unos brotes de frijol; sirva caliente.*

□　*El olor fresco del jugo de limón es perfecto para el pescado. No sólo quita cualquier olor desagradable del pescado sino que añade vitamina C a la comida.*

醋椒魚　　　**Yellow Croaker & Vinegar**

Roncador Amarillo en Vinagre

黃魚（圖1）1條 . 450公克（12兩）

① 蔥末 1大匙
　 薑末 1小匙

② 高湯或水 5杯
　 酒 .... ½ 大匙
　 鹽 1小匙
　 味精 .... ¼ 小匙

③ 醋 2大匙
　 胡椒粉 .... ½ 小匙
　 麻油 1小匙

④ 蔥絲 2大匙
　 香菜 2大匙

🐟　　🐟　　🐟

1 yellow croaker (Fig.1),
　1lb.(450g)

① 1 T. minced green onions
　1 t. minced ginger root

② 5 c. stock or water
　½ T. cooking wine, 1 t. salt

③ 2 T. vinegar, ½ t. pepper
　1 t. sesame oil

④ 2 T. shredded green onion
　2 T. coriander

🐟　　🐟　　🐟

1 roncador amarillo (Fig. 1),
　1 lb. (450g)

① 1 C. cebollín finamente picado
　1 c. raíz de jengibre finamente
　picada

② 5 tz. caldo o agua
　½ C. vino para cocinar, 1 c. sal

③ 2 C. vinagre, ½ c. pimienta
　1 c. aceite de sésamo

④ 2 C. cebollín rallado
　2 C. cilantro

1️⃣ 魚在兩面肉厚處各斜劃二、三刀，將 ③ 料置大湯碗中備用。

2️⃣ 油1大匙燒熱，炒香 ① 料，隨入 ② 料煮開後，放入魚待滾，改中火蓋鍋燜煮約6分鐘，趁熱倒入湯碗內，並撒上 ④ 料即可。

☐ 此道菜為北方一道具特色之魚湯，湯鮮味香，值得一嚐。

🐟　　🐟　　🐟

1️⃣ Score fish diagonally in the thick areas; mix ③ in a large deep bowl; set aside.

2️⃣ Heat 1 T. oil; stir-fry ① until fragrant; add ② ; bring to boil; add fish; bring to boil again; reduce heat to medium; cook about 6 minutes; while hot, pour into the soup bowl; sprinkle with ④ ; serve.

☐ This dish has a northern Chinese flair. This is a delicious and aromatic dish.

🐟　　🐟　　🐟

1️⃣ *Haga cortes diagonales en las áreas gruesas del pescado; mezcle ③ en un tazón grande y hondo; deje aparte.*

2️⃣ *Caliente 1 C. de aceite; fría-revolviendo ① hasta que esté aromático; agregue ② ; haga hervir; agregue el pescado; haga hervir de nuevo; reduzca el fuego a moderado; cocine como 6 minutos; mientras está caliente, vacíe en el tazón de sopa; espolvoree con ④ ; sirva.*

☐ *Este platillo tiene el estilo del norte de China. Es un platillo delicioso y aromático.*

1

味噌魚湯　　**Fish Fillets & Miso Sauce**

Filetes de Pescado en Salsa Miso

4人份 · serves 4
4 porciones

魚肉 .... 150公克（4兩）
豆腐2塊 .... 300公克（8兩）
味噌 4大匙
蔥花 2大匙

① 水 5杯
糖 .... ¼ 小匙
味精或鰹魚粉 .... ¼ 小匙

    ❧　　❧　　❧

⅓ lb.(150g) fish fillet
2 bean curd, ⅔ lb.(300g)
4 T. miso
2 T. chopped green onion

① 5 c. water
¼ t. sugar
¼ t. dashi

    ❧　　❧　　❧

⅓ lb. (150g) filete de pescado
2 pedazos tofu, ⅔ lb. (300g)
4 C. miso
2 C. cebollín picado

① 5 tz. agua
¼ c. azúcar
¼ c. dashi

1　魚肉切丁或長方塊，豆腐亦切丁備用。

2　①料燒開，入魚肉、豆腐煮開，隨入味噌煮滾即刻熄火撒上蔥花即可。

□　鮮魚亦可改用魚頭、魚骨或小魚乾，但需於水開後以中火續煮約10分鐘。味噌以網入鍋（圖1）較易散開。

    ❧　　❧　　❧

1　Dice fish or cut into rectangular shapes. Dice the bean curd; set aside.

2　Bring ① to boil; add fish and bean curd; bring to boil; add miso; bring to another boil; sprinkle with green onions; serve.

□　Fish head, fish bones, or diced small fish may be substituted for fish fillets. After bring ① to boil, continue cooking 10 minutes over medium heat. To dissolve miso easily, put miso in a net then put the net into the pot (Fig. 1).

    ❧　　❧　　❧

1　*Corte el pescado en pedazos de cubo o de rectángulo. Corte el tofu en cubos; deje aparte.*

2　*Haga hervir ① ; agregue el pescado y el tofu; haga hervir; agregue el miso; haga hervir de nuevo; espolvoree con cebollines; sirva.*

□　*Los filetes de pescado pueden substituirse por cabeza de pescado, espinazo de pescado, o pescado pequeño en cubitos. Cambie el tiempo de la cocción a 10 minutos a fuego moderado cuando empiece a hervir. Para deshacer el miso con facilidad, póngalo en una red luego ponga la red en la olla (Fig. 1).*

1

Pez Comestible y Ajo

虱目魚（圖1）450公克（12兩）
蒜 10粒

① 高湯或水 5杯
鹽 1小匙
味精 .... ¼小匙
酒 1大匙
薑絲 2大匙

🐟　　🐟　　🐟

1 lb.(450g) milkfish (Fig. 1)
10 garlic cloves

① 5 c. stock or water
1 t. salt
1 T. cooking wine
2 T. shredded ginger root

🐟　　🐟　　🐟

*1 lb. (450g) pez comestible
　(Fig. 1)
10 dientes de ajo*

① *5 tz. caldo o agua
1 c. sal
1 C. vino para cocinar
2 C. raíz de jengibre rallada*

1 魚切段，蒜稍拍同置燉碗中，加 ① 料，水開後以大火蒸約30分鐘即可。

☐ 亦可以電鍋蒸熟或在爐上直接以鍋將 ① 料燒開後，入魚煮滾，續以小火煮約15分鐘。

🐟　　🐟　　🐟

1 Cut fish in sections; crush garlic lightly; place with fish in a steaming bowl; add ① ; Bring water for steaming to boil; steam fish over high heat 30 minutes.

☐ This dish is best cooked in a steamer. It also can be cooked on the stove as follows: Bring ① to boil; add fish; return to boil; continue cooking over low heat for about 15 minutes.

🐟　　🐟　　🐟

1 *Corte el pescado en secciones; machaque el ajo ligeramente; coloque con el pescado en un tazón para hervir; agregue ① ; haga hervir el agua; para cocer el pescado al vapor sobre fuego alto por 30 minutos.*

☐ *Este platillo se cocina mejor en una vaporera. También se puede cocinar en la estufa de la siguiente manera: Haga hervir ① ; agregue el pescado; vuelva a hervir; continúe cocinando a fuego lento como 15 minutos.*

1

鱸魚苦瓜湯　Perch & Melon Soup

Sopa de Róbalo y Melón

serves 4
4 porciones

鱸魚 .... 450公克（12兩）
苦瓜 1條

高湯 6杯
酒 2大匙
小魚乾 2大匙
豆豉 .... ⅔大匙
蒜末 .... ½大匙
鹽 1½小匙

🐚　　🐚　　🐚

1 lb. (450g) perch (sea bass)
1 bitter melon

6 c. stock
2 T. cooking wine
2 T. dried small fish
⅔ T. fermented black
beans
½ T. minced garlic cloves
1½ t. salt

🐚　　🐚　　🐚

1 lb. (450g) róbalo
1 melón agrio

6 tz. caldo
2 C. vino para cocinar
2 C. pescado seco pequeño
⅔ C. frijoles negros
fermentados
½ C. dientes de ajo finamente
picados
1½ c. sal

1️⃣ 鱸魚去鱗、除鰓洗淨切大塊，苦瓜去籽切塊。

2️⃣ ❶ 料置鍋燒開，入苦瓜煮約15分鐘後，加鱸魚同煮5分鐘即成。

☐ 也可將鱸魚、苦瓜分別入開水川燙後，全部材料放入燉盅內蒸30分鐘即可趁熱食用。

🐚　　🐚　　🐚

1️⃣ Scale perch; remove gills; clean and cut into large pieces; seed melon.

2️⃣ Bring ❶ to boil; add melon and cook for about 15 minutes; add perch; cook for another 5 minutes; serve.

☐ You can also blanch perch and melon separately; transfer them with other ingredients into a covered, steaming bowl; steam for 30 minutes; serve hot.

🐚　　🐚　　🐚

1️⃣ *Descame el pescado; quítele las branquias; lave y corte en pedazos grandes; quítele las semillas al melón.*

2️⃣ *Haga hervir ❶ ; agregue el melón y cueza como 15 minutos; agregue el pescado; cocine por otros 5 minutos más; sirva.*

☐ *También se puede sumergir en agua hirviendo el pescado y el melón por separado; vacíelos con los otros ingredientes al tazón en que se va a cocer y tape; cueza al vapor por 30 minutos; sirva caliente.*

活河鰻2條 .. 約600公克（1斤）

① 蔥白 6小段
　 薑 4片
　 枸杞 1大匙
　 當歸 2片

② 水 5杯
　 酒 1杯
　 鹽 1¼小匙
　 味精 .... 少許

🐟　　🐟　　🐟

2 live river eels, 1⅓ lbs.
　(600g)

① 6 white part of green onion
　　sections
　4 slices ginger root
　1 T. dried boxphorn fruit
　　(kei chi)
　2 slices dang guei
　　(Chinese angelica)

② 5 c. water
　1 c. cooking wine
　1¼ t. salt

🐟　　🐟　　🐟

2 anguilas de río vivas, 1⅓ lbs.
　(600g)

① 6 secciones de la parte blanca
　　de cebollines
　4 rebanadas raíz de jengibre
　1 C. fruta seca boxphorn (kei
　　chi)
　2 rebanadas dang guei

② 5 tz. agua
　1 tz. vino para cocinar
　1¼ c. sal

1

2

枸杞燉鰻　Steamed Eel & Boxphorn Fruit
Anguila y Fruta Seca al Vapor

4人份 · serves 4
4 porciones

① 河鰻處理乾淨，切4公分長段。① 料置燉盅內，再入鰻魚及 ② 料，放入蒸鍋內蒸1小時即可。

☐ 活河鰻處理法：先剁斷河鰻頭部擱置片刻見其不滾動時淋上開水（圖1），去除鰻皮上之白濁物（圖2）。活河鰻之內臟味道很好，可一起燉食，但要先拿掉膽囊。

🐟　　🐟　　🐟

① Clean eel; cut into 1½" (4cm) sections. Place ① in a steaming bowl; add eel and ② to bowl; steam for 1 hour; serve.

☐ To prepare a live eel: Cut off head; set aside until eel stops moving; pour on boiling water (Fig. 1); remove white residue off the eel's skin (Fig. 2). Eel's intestines are flavorful. They can be cooked with the flesh. Remove gall bladder before cooking.

🐟　　🐟　　🐟

① Limpie las anguilas; corte en secciones de 1½" (4cm). Coloque ① en un tazón para cocer al vapor; agregue las anguilas y ② al tazón; cueza al vapor por 1 hora; sirva.

☐ Para preparar anguila viva: Córtele la cabeza; deje aparte hasta que la anguila deje de moverse; vacíele agua hirviendo (Fig. 1); retire el residuo blanco de la piel de la anguila (Fig. 2). Los intestinos de anguila tienen mucho sabor. Se pueden cocer con la carne. Retírele la bilis antes de cocinar el pescado.

酸辣魚羹　Spicy & Sour Fish Soup

Sopa Agridulce de Pescado

魚肉 .... 150公克（4兩）
蛋 1個
① 酒、太白粉 .... 各½大匙
② 豆腐絲、木耳絲、紅蘿蔔絲 ......
.... 各1杯
水 5杯
③ 鹽 .....¾小匙，醋 3大匙
胡椒、糖 .... 各½小匙
醬油 1大匙
④ 太白粉、水 各3大匙
⑤ 蔥花 1大匙
香菜 .... 隨意

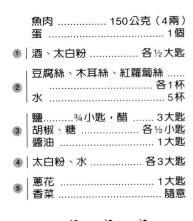

ક   ક   ક

⅓ lb.(150g) fish fillet
1 egg

① ½ T. ea.: cooking wine,
cornstarch

② 1 c. ea.(shredded): bean
curd, dried wood ears,
carrots
5 c. water

③ ¾ t.salt, 3 T. vinegar
½ t. ea.: pepper, sugar
1 T. soy sauce

④ 3 T. ea.: cornstarch, water

⑤ 1 T. chopped green onions
coriander as desired

ક   ક   ક

⅓ lb. (150g) filete de pescado
1 huevo

① *½ C. c/u: vino para cocinar,*
maicena

② *1 tz. c/u, (rallado): tofu, orejas*
de madera secas, zanahorias
5 tz. agua

③ *¾ c. sal, 3 C. vinagre*
½ c. c/u: pimienta, azúcar
1 C. salsa de soya

④ *3 C. c/u: maicena, agua*

⑤ *1 C. cebollín picado*
cilantro al gusto

1　魚肉切粗絲，調 ① 料拌勻備用。

2　將 ② 料燒開，改中火入魚肉輕輕攪開，燒開後加 ③ 料調味，並以拌勻的 ④ 料勾芡後，徐徐淋入打勻的蛋液，略攪拌成絲狀，即刻熄火撒上 ⑤ 料即成。

ક   ક   ક

1　Cut fish into thick strips; marinate in ① thoroughly; set aside.

2　Bring ② to boil; reduce heat to medium; cook and stir gently to separate fish strips; bring to boil; season with ③ ; thicken with mixture ④ ; slowly pour beaten egg mixture into the soup in a thin stream while stirring gently; turn off heat immediately; sprinkle with ⑤ ; serve.

ક   ક   ક

1　*Corte el pescado en tiras gruesas; marine en ① completamente; deje aparte.*

2　*Haga hervir ② ; reduzca el fuego a moderado; cocine y revuelva ligeramente para separar las tiras de pescado; haga hervir; sazone con ③ ; espese con la mezcla ④ ; despacio vacíe el huevo batido en la sopa en forma de una tira delgada mientras lo revuelve cuidadosamente; apague el fuego inmediatamente; espolvoree con ⑤ ; sirva.*

香菇魚羹　Mushrooms & Fish Paste Soup
Sopa de Hongos y Pasta de Pescado

土托魚肉 .... 225公克（6兩）
地瓜粉或太白粉 3大匙
「炸油」 3杯

① 醬油、酒 .... 各½大匙
　　糖.......1小匙，蒜末 1大匙

② 大白菜 .... 450公克（12兩）
　　香菇2朵·紅蘿蔔絲75公克（2兩）

③ 高湯或水 4杯
　　鹽、糖 各1小匙

④ 太白粉、水 各3大匙

⑤ 黑醋、醬油 各1大匙
　　胡椒、麻油 ... 適量，香菜 .. 隨意

½ lb. (225g) barred spanish
   mackerel
3 T. sweet potato powder or
   cornstarch
3 c. oil for deep-frying

① ½ T. ea.: soy sauce,
    cooking wine
   1 t. sugar
   1 T. minced garlic cloves

② 1 lb. (450g) nappa cabbage
   2 Chinese black mushrooms
   2½ oz.(75g) shredded carrots

③ 4 c. stock or water
   1 t. ea.: salt, sugar

④ 3 T. ea.: cornstarch, water

⑤ 1 T. ea.: black vinegar, soy
    sauce
   pepper, sesame oil,
    coriander as desired

½ lb. (225g) caballa
3 C. polvo de camote o maicena
3 tz. aceite para freír

① *½ C. c/u: salsa de soya, vino*
    para cocinar
   1 c. azúcar
   1 C. dientes de ajo finamente
    picados

② *1 lb. (450g) repollo napa*
   2 hongos chinos negros
   2½ oz. (75g) zanahoria rallada

③ *4 tz. caldo o agua*
   1 c. c/u: sal, azúcar

④ *3 C. c/u: maicena, agua*

⑤ *1 C. c/u: vinagre negro, salsa*
    de soya
   pimienta, aceite de sésamo,
    cilantro al gusto

1 魚肉切塊調 ① 料醃20分鐘，炸前瀝乾拌地瓜粉。大白菜切塊，香菇泡軟切絲。

2 「炸油」燒熱，入魚塊以中火炸約3分鐘呈金黃色並熟撈起（圖1）。③ 料燒開，入 ② 料煮軟，以拌勻 ④ 料勾芡，加入魚塊及 ⑤ 料即可。

□ 炸熟魚塊可直接食用或冷凍保存一個月，隨時取用，是理想的便當菜。

1 Cut fish into pieces; marinate in ① for 20 minutes; drain and coat with sweet potato powder before deep-frying. Cut cabbage into pieces; soften Chinese black mushroom in water then shred.

2 Heat oil for deep-frying; deep-fry fish over medium heat until done and golden, about 3 minutes (Fig. 1); remove. Bring ③ to boil; add ②; cook until softened; add mixture ④ to thicken; return fish and add ⑤; serve.

□ Deep-fried fish can be served right away or kept frozen for up to 1 month. This dish is ideal for packed lunch.

1 *Corte el pescado en pedazos, marine en ① por 20 minutos; escurra y reboce con el polvo de camote antes de freír. Corte el repollo en pedazos, ablande los hongos negros chinos en agua, luego rállelos.*

2 *Caliente el aceite para freír; fría el pescado en una sartén a fuego moderado hasta que esté listo y dorado, como 3 minutos (Fig. 1); retire. Haga hervir ③; agregue ②; cocine hasta que se ablande; agregue la mezcla ④ para espesar; regrese el pescado y agregue ⑤; sirva.*

□ *El pescado frito se puede servir inmediatamente o se puede congelar hasta por 1 mes. Este platillo es ideal para llevar de almuerzo.*

油條魚羹　Fish Soup & Chinese Crullers

Sopa de Pescado y Churros Chinos

魚肉 .... 150公克（4兩）
油條（切小塊）................. 1條
筍（切小片）..................... 1杯
芹菜末 .... ½ 杯
蛋 1個

① 酒、太白粉 .... 各½ 大匙

② 高湯或水 5杯
　 鹽 1小匙
　 味精、胡椒 .... 各¼ 小匙

③ 太白粉、水 各3大匙

🦐　　🦐　　🦐

⅓ lb.(150g) fish fillet
1 Chinese cruller, cut in pieces
1 c. bamboo shoots, sliced
½ c. chopped Chinese celery
1 egg

① **½ T. cooking wine**
　 ½ T. cornstarch

② **5 c. stock or water**
　 1 t. salt
　 ¼ t. pepper

③ **3 T. ea.: cornstarch, water**

🦐　　🦐　　🦐

⅓ lb. (150g) filete de pescado
1 churro chino cortado en pedazos
1 tz. brotes de bambú, en rebanadas
½ tz. apio chino picado
1 huevo

① *½ C. vino para cocinar*
　 ½ C. maicena

② *5 tz. caldo o agua*
　 1 c. sal
　 ¼ c. pimienta

③ *3 C. c/u: maicena, agua*

1 魚肉切小丁調 ① 料，油條炸酥或烤酥置湯碗中備用。

2 ② 料燒開，入筍片以中火煮約10分鐘後，加魚肉輕輕攪開，隨入芹菜末並以 ③ 料勾芡後徐徐淋入打勻的蛋液，略攪拌成絲狀，倒入湯碗中，食時加上油條即可。

☐ 油條（或炸麵包丁）為保持酥脆較香，故宜在食用前才加。

🦐　　🦐　　🦐

1 Dice fish and marinate in ① . Deep-fry or bake Chinese cruller until crispy; place in a large bowl; set aside.

2 Bring ② to boil; add bamboo shoots; cook about 10 minutes over medium heat; add fish; cook and gently stir to separate diced fish; add Chinese celery; thicken the mixture with ③ ; slowly add beaten egg mixture into the soup in a thin stream while stirring gently; pour into a large soup bowl; sprinkle with cruller when serving.

☐ Chinese crullers (or croutons) taste better when crisp. Add to the soup just before serving to maintain crispiness.

🦐　　🦐　　🦐

1 *Corte el pescado en cubos y marine en ① . Fría u hornee el churro chino hasta que esté crujiente; coloque en un tazón grande; deje aparte.*

2 *Haga hervir ② ; agregue los brotes de bambú; cocine como 10 minutos a fuego moderado; agregue el pescado; cocine y revuelva con cuidado para separar los cubos de pescado; agregue el apio chino; espese la mezcla con ③ ; despacio agregue la mezcla de huevo batido a la sopa en una tira delgada mientras lo revuelve cuidadosamente; vacíe en un tazón de sopa grande; espolvoree con los churros chinos al servir.*

☐ *Los churros chinos saben mejor crujientes. Agréguelos a la sopa cuando la vaya a servir para mantenerlos crujientes.*

Sopa de Pescado Pequeño

銀魚（魩仔魚）或
　其他魚肉切絲　225公克(6兩)
嫩豆腐（切絲）.................. 1杯
蔥絲 2大匙
麻油 1小匙

① 紅蘿蔔絲、筍絲 .... 各½杯
　香菇絲（或木耳絲）......... ¼杯

② 高湯或水 6杯
　酒 1大匙
　鹽 1½小匙

③ 太白粉 .... 4大匙，水 6大匙

🍃　　🍃　　🍃

½ lb.(225g) small fish or
　other shredded fish
　fillets
1 c. shredded soft bean
　curd
2 T. shredded green
　onions
1 t. sesame oil

① ½ c. ea.(shredded):
　carrots, bamboo shoots
　¼ c. shredded Chinese
　black mushrooms (or
　dried wood ears)

② 6 c. stock or water
　1 T. cooking wine,1½ t. salt

③ 4 T. cornstarch, 6 T. water

🍃　　🍃　　🍃

*½ lb. (225g) pescado pequeño
u otros filetes de pescado,
rallados
1 tz. tofu suave rallado
2 C. cebollín rallado
1 c. aceite de sésamo*

① *½ tz. c/u (rallado): zanahoria,
brotes de bambú
¼ tz. hongos negros chinos
rallados (u orejas de madera
secas)*

② *6 tz. caldo o agua
1 C. vino para cocinar, 1½ c. sal*

③ *4 C. maicena, 6 C. agua*

1

① 銀魚洗淨瀝乾。② 料燒開（如使用熟銀魚因已有鹹味，鹽需酌減），入① 料煮4分鐘後以 ③ 料勾成薄汁，再加豆腐及銀魚，燒開後撒上蔥及麻油即可。

② 湯内也可加蛋花，喜酸辣味者可再加醬油2大匙、醋3大匙、胡椒½小匙。

銀魚粥　米1杯加水8杯、鹽1小匙、酒1大匙燒開後，改小火煮20分鐘再加銀魚150公克（4兩）燒開即可。食時撒上紫菜、柴魚（圖1）、蔥花及香菜。

🍃　　🍃　　🍃

① Clean fish; drain. Bring ② to boil (reduce salt, if using ready-made salty fish); add ① ; cook for 4 minutes; stir in ③ to thicken the mixture; add bean curd and fish; bring to boil; sprinkle with green onions and sesame oil; serve.

② If desired, add beaten egg mixture into the soup. For extra sour and spicy flavor, add 2 T. soy sauce, 3 T. vinegar, and ½ t. black pepper.

Small Fish Porridge　Add 8 c. water, 1 t. salt, and 1 T. wine to 1 c. rinsed rice; bring to boil; reduce to low heat; cook for 20 minutes; add ⅓ lb. (150g) small fish; bring to boil again; serve. When serving, sprinkle with nori, dashi (Fig. 1), green onions, and coriander.

🍃　　🍃　　🍃

① *Lave el pescado; escurra. Haga hervir ② (reduzca la sal, si usa pescado salado ya preparado); agregue ① ; cocine por 4 minutos; agregue ③ revolviendo para espesar la mezcla; agregue el tofu y pescado; haga hervir; vacíe con cebollines y aceite de sésamo; sirva.*

② *Si gusta, agregue la mezcla de huevo batido a la sopa. Para un sabor más sazonado, agregue 2 C. salsa de soya, 3 C. vinagre, y ½ c. pimienta negra.*

Potaje de Pescado Pequeño *Agregue 8 tz. agua, 1 c. sal, y 1 C. vino a 1 tz. de arroz enjuagado; haga hervir; reduzca el fuego a lento; cocine por 20 minutos; agregue ⅓ lb. (150g) pescado pequeño; haga hervir de nuevo; sirva. Cuando lo sirva, espolvoree con nori, dashi (Fig. 1), cebollín y cilantro.*

93

蘿蔔魚湯　　　　Fish & Carrot Soup

Sopa de Pescado y Zanahoria

4人份 · serves 4
4 porciones

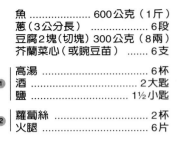

魚	....	600公克（1斤）
蔥（3公分長）	....	6段
豆腐2塊(切塊)300公克（8兩）		
芥蘭菜心（或豌豆苗）	....	6支

①
高湯	....	6杯
酒	....	2大匙
鹽	....	1½小匙

②
蘿蔔絲	....	2杯
火腿	....	6片

🍃　　🍃　　🍃

1⅓ lbs. (600g) fish
6 green onion sections,
  1¼" (3cm)
2 bean curd (cut in pieces),
  ⅔ lb. (300g)
6 Chinese broccoli stems
  or snow pea leaves

①
6 c. stock
2 T. cooking wine
1½ t. salt

②
2 c. shredded carrots
6 ham slices

🍃　　🍃　　🍃

1⅓ lbs. (600g) pescado
6 secciones de cebollín, 1¼"
  (3cm)
2 pedazos tofu (cortado en
  pedazos), ⅔ lb. (300g)
6 tallos de bróculi chino u
  hojas de chícharos chinos

①
6 tz. caldo
2 C. vino para cocinar
1½ c. sal

②
2 tz. zanahoria rallada
6 rebanadas de jamón

1 　魚在肉厚處劃刀痕，拭乾。油3大匙燒熱，將魚煎呈微黃取出。

2 　油1大匙燒熱，炒香蔥段，隨入 **①** 料煮開，加 **②** 料及魚再煮10分鐘（去除表面油質及泡沫使湯較清），續加豆腐煮3分鐘後放入芥蘭菜再燒開即可。

☐ 　如魚非常新鮮，可以不煎直接放入湯內，但煎或炸過的魚，湯味較香。

🍃　　🍃　　🍃

1 Score fish in thick areas; pat dry. Heat 3 T. oil; pan-fry fish until lightly browned; remove.

2 Heat 1 T. oil; stir-fry green onions; add **①**; bring to boil. Add **②** and return fish; cook for 10 minutes (skim grease and foam from surface to make soup clear). Add bean curd; cook for 3 minutes. Add broccoli; bring to boil; serve.

☐ If fish is very fresh, pan-frying may be omitted. However, pan-fried or deep-fried fish adds more flavor to the soup.

🍃　　🍃　　🍃

1 *Haga cortes en las áreas gruesas del pescado; seque ligeramente. Caliente 3 C. de aceite; fría en la sartén hasta que esté poco dorado; retire.*

2 *Caliente 1 C. de aceite; fría-revolviendo el cebollín; agregue **①**; haga hervir. Agregue **②** y regrese el pescado; cocine por 10 minutos (con una cuchara quítele la grasa y la espuma de la superficie para hacer la sopa clara). Agregue el tofu; cocine por 3 minutos. Agregue el bróculi; haga hervir; sirva.*

☐ *Si el pescado está muy fresco, no es necesario freírlo en la sartén. Sin embargo, el pescado sofrito o frito le da más sabor a la sopa.*

94

鹹魚炒飯　Fried Rice with Salted Fish

Arroz Frito con Pescado Salado

鹹魚 .... 150公克（4兩）
蝦仁 .... 225公克（6兩）
蔥花 .... ½杯

① 鹽 .... ¼小匙
酒 1小匙
蛋白 .... ½個
太白粉 .... ¾大匙

② 青豆仁 .... ½杯
洋菇或草菇 .... ½杯

③ 飯 6杯
味精、胡椒 .... 各少許

⅓ lb.(150g) salted fish
½ lb.(225g) shelled shrimp
½ c. chopped green onions

① ¼ t. salt
1 t. cooking wine
½ egg white
¾ T. cornstarch

② ½ c. green peas
½ c. mushrooms or straw mushrooms

③ 6 c. cooked rice
dash of pepper

⅓ lb. (150g) pescado salado
½ lb. (225g) camarón pelado
½ tz. cebollines picados

① ¼ c. sal
1 c. vino para cocinar
½ clara de huevo
¾ C. maicena

② ½ tz. chícharos
½ tz. hongos u hongos con tallo

③ 6 tz. arroz cocido
pizca de pimienta

① 蝦仁加鹽½小匙略抓拌後用清水沖洗數次，瀝乾後依序調入 ① 料拌勻，炒前拌油1大匙則炒時蝦仁較易鏟開。

② 油½杯燒熱，放入蝦仁翻炒至熟撈出。留油2大匙放入鹹魚兩面煎黃盛起，剔除骨刺壓碎（圖1）。

③ 油3大匙燒熱，炒香蔥花續入 ② 料略炒，再入鹹魚、蝦及 ③ 料炒勻即可。

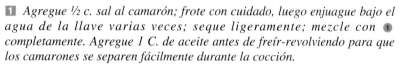

① Add ½ t. salt to shrimp; rub gently then rinse under running water several times; pat dry; mix in ① thoroughly. Mix in 1 T. oil before stir-frying to separate shrimp easily during cooking.

② Heat ½ c. oil; stir-fry shrimp until done; remove. Ladle off and reserve 2 T. oil in pan; pan-fry salted fish until golden on both sides; remove. Remove fish bones; smash the fish (Fig. 1).

③ Heat 3 T. oil; stir-fry green onions until fragrant; stir in ② briefly; add salted fish, shrimp, and ③; cook until combined; serve.

① *Agregue ½ c. sal al camarón; frote con cuidado, luego enjuague bajo el agua de la llave varias veces; seque ligeramente; mezcle con ① completamente. Agregue 1 C. de aceite antes de freír-revolviendo para que los camarones se separen fácilmente durante la cocción.*

② *Caliente ½ tz. de aceite; fría-revolviendo los camarones hasta que estén listos; retire. Saque el aceite dejando 2 C. de aceite en la sartén; fría el pescado salado hasta que esté dorado por ambos lados; retire. Quítele las espinas al pescado; muela el pescado (Fig. 1).*

③ *Caliente 3 C. de aceite; fría-revolviendo los cebollines hasta que estén aromáticos; agregue ② revolviendo brevemente; agregue el pescado salado, camarones y ③; cocine hasta que se combine; sirva.*

1

COOKBOOKS :

ALL COOKBOOKS ARE BILINGUAL (ENGLISH/CHINESE) UNLESS FOOTNOTED OTHERWISE

Apetizers, Chinese Style
Chinese Appetizers & Garnishes
Chinese Cooking, Favorite Home Dishes
Chinese Cooking For Beginners (Rev.)[1]
Chinese Cooking Made Easy
Chinese Cuisine
Chinese Cuisine-Cantonese Style
Chinese Cuisine-Shanghai Style
Chinese Cuisine-Szechwan Style
Chinese Cuisine-Taiwanese Style
Chinese Dim Sum
Chinese Herb Cooking for Health
Chinese Home Cooking for Health
Chinese One Dish Meals (Rev.)[3]
Chinese Snacks (Rev.)
Favorite Chinese Dishes
Fish[3]

Great Garnishes
Healthful Cooking
Indian Cuisine
International Baking Delights
Japanese Cuisine
Low Cholesterol Chinese Cuisine
Mexican Cooking Made Easy[4]
Noodles, Chinese Home-Cooking
Noodles, Classical Chinese Cooking
One Dish Meals; From Popular Cuisines[3]
Rice, Chinese Home-Cooking
Rice, Traditional Chinese Cooking
Shellfish[3]
Simply Vegetarian
Thai Cooking Made Easy
Vegetarian Cooking

SMALL COOKBOOK SERIES

Beef[2]
Chicken[2]
Soup! Soup! Soup!
Tofu! Tofu! Tofu!
Vegetables[2]
Very! Very! Vegetarian!

VIDEOS

Chinese Garnishes I[5]
Chinese Garnishes II[5]
Chinese Stir-Frying: Beef[5]
Chinese Stir-Frying: Chicken[5]
Chinese Stir-Frying: Vegetables[5]

OTHERS

Carving Tools

---

1 Also available in English/Spanish, French/Chinese, and German/Chinese
2 English and Chinese are in separate editions
3 Trilingual English/Chinese/Spanish edition
4 Also available in English/Spanish
5 English Only

Wei-Chuan Cookbooks can be purchased in the U.S.A., Canada and twenty other countries worldwide
1455 Monterey Pass Road, #110, Monterey Park, CA 91754, U.S.A. • Tel: (213)261-3880 • Fax: (213) 261-3299

味全叢書

食譜系列

(如無數字標註，即為中英對照版)

美味小菜
拼盤與盤飾
實用家庭菜
實用中國菜(修訂版)[1]
速簡中國菜
中國菜
廣東菜
上海菜
四川菜

台灣菜
飲茶食譜
養生藥膳
養生家常菜
簡餐專輯(修訂版)[3]
點心專輯
家常100
魚[3]
盤飾精選

健康食譜
印度菜
實用烘焙
日本料理
均衡飲食
墨西哥菜[4]
麵，家常篇
麵，精華篇
簡餐(五國風味)[3]

米食，家常篇
米食，傳統篇
蝦、貝、蟹[3]
健康素
泰國菜
素食

味全小食譜

牛肉[2]   湯
雞肉[2]   豆腐
蔬菜[2]   家常素食

錄影帶

盤飾 I[5]   炒菜入門，牛肉[5]
盤飾 II[5]   炒菜入門，雞肉[5]
               炒菜入門，蔬菜[5]

其他

雕花刀

---

1 中英、英西、中法、中德版   2 中文版及英文版   3 中、英、西對照版   4 英西版   5 英文版

味全食譜在台、美加及全球二十餘國皆有發行 • 味全出版社有限公司 • 台北市仁愛路4段28號2樓
Tel:(02)2702-1148 • Fax:(02)2704-2729

OTROS LIBROS DE WEI-CHUAN

EDICIONES EN ESPAÑOL

Cocina China Para Principiantes, Edición Revisada[1]
Cocina Popular de Un Solo Platillo[2]
Comida China de Un Solo Platillo, Edición Revisada[2]
Comida Mexicana, Fácil de Preparar[3]
Mariscos, Estilo Chino Fácil de Preparar[2]
Pescado, Estilo Chino Fácil de Preparar[2]

---

1 Disponible en Inglés/Español, Inglés/Chino, Francés/Chino, y Alemán/Chino
2 Edición trilingüe Inglés/Chino/Español
3 Disponible en ediciones bilingües Inglés/Español e Inglés/Chino

Los Libros de Cocina Wei-Chuan se pueden comprar en E.E.U.U., Canadá y otros 20 países a través del mundo.
1455 Monterey Pass Road, #110, Monterey Park, CA 91754, U.S.A. • Tel: (213)261-3880 • Fax: (213) 261-3299